THE
CONQUEROR'S
WAY

A **SIMPLE** PLAYBOOK FOR VICTORIOUS PURSUIT

JEREMY BARKEY

credo
house publishers

The Conqueror's Way
Copyright © 2025 by Jeremy Barkey
All rights reserved.

Published in the United States by Credo House Publishers
a division of Credo Communications, LLC, Grand Rapids, MI
credohousepublishers.com

ISBN: 978-1-62586-301-0

Editing by Donna Huisjen
Cover and interior design by Frank Gutbrod

Printed in the United States of America
First edition

To the family I have been put on this earth to
lead, serve, and sacrifice for:
my children, Isabella, Landon, and Ellie;
and my wife, Samantha.

Kids: Life won't be easy, but it can be wonderful.
I give you these simple fundamentals
to guide your pursuit of God's best for you.

Samantha: Thank you for your love, partnership,
and patience. I could not have started or finished
this work without you.

I love you all.

"Hallelujah!
Salvation and glory and power
belong to our God."
REVELATION 19:1

CONTENTS

PREFACE

WHY THE CONQUEROR'S WAY?

"Truth is found in simplicity, not in the multiplication and confusion of things."

SIR ISAAC NEWTON

Who am I?

Why are we here?

Where am I going?

Where did I come from?

Why do I feel anxious?

How can I be courageous?

What should I be doing with my life?

Am I using my gifts the way I should?

Do I have good friends?

Am I loved?

Why do we experience pain?

When will my suffering end?

Does God really exist?

If so, can I trust Him?

Have you ever found yourself asking these or related questions? If you're like me, the answer is yes. Fact is, to live a life without conviction and belief regarding the answers to these questions is to live a life that is destined for dissatisfying emptiness instead of the lasting fulfillment our souls long and thirst for. Addressing this human reality, as well as identifying and overcoming the obstacles we encounter in pursuit of fulfillment, is what *The Conqueror's Way* is about. While the simple framework offered in this book *will* point you toward a better way of living, creating a better version of yourself in the process, it more importantly points you to the One and only Source from which these questions meet their answers. A source that never fails to satisfy our thirst for wholeness, even amid our human struggle and striving.

With that said, by walking in the Conqueror's Way we come to understand what it is to maximize our unique gifts, for the benefit of others, and live in abundant peace, joy, and freedom as we grow to become people of strength and light who reflect the heart of a loving God. But how? Before we answer that, I want to be genuinely transparent about a few things . . .

First, my aim is to offer a framework for understanding six situational themes this life presents to each of us. Within this framework I'll point to the Source that provides the Way for experiencing fulfillment (defined by the peace, joy, and freedom our souls long for) and offer basic daily fundamentals for growing through the challenges we encounter in our human reality.

Again, while we will discover our "best version" as we engage in this pursuit, this is *not* for our own personal gain or glory but to bring glory back to the loving Source and Creator who created and sustains us. Additionally, I will supplement the Conqueror's Way framework by sharing life lessons learned with as little "shoulding" as possible. At the end of the day, my offerings are mere invitations to realize this vision of *effective living* by discovering, developing, and using the gifts we've each been given by God, which are refined through our struggle, pain, and suffering, for the benefit of others in accordance with our Creator's design.

Furthermore, essential in this pursuit is an awareness that none of us is asked to walk the Conqueror's Way alone. The same loving Creator who charted your course and wants to meet your deepest needs is *with* you all the way and wants you to live *from* His victory. The simple reality is that we cannot experience real peace, joy, and freedom (victory) in our lives, no matter how much stuff we accumulate, wealth we amass, or accomplishments we achieve apart from the will and power of the One who authored those blessings. When we search for God with *all* our heart, soul, mind, and strength and embrace the laws that reveal how His world works, we are free to grow in His ways as we practice the daily application of His truth. Simple, right? While simple does not equate to easy, walking the Conqueror's Way is the most rewarding thing you'll ever do.

Second, I'd like to acknowledge that I believe in the God of the Holy Trinity (God the Father, Jesus Christ the Son, and the Holy Spirit). With that said, this book is not about living *religiously*. In fact, I'd be the first to tell anyone that the pursuit of religion leads to emptiness and dissatisfaction. I know this from experience and have zero interest in sending others down a legalistic, rule-following rabbit hole. Discovering a loving relationship with the risen Jesus Christ who is *the* Conqueror, on the other hand, will bring about a growth that will transform your life. Therefore, I will share what I've learned in my journey of *working out* the salvation that my loving God freely provides for me as His child.

Finally, while I aim to share hope and light in this book, I recognize that I am an imperfect human who, in my flesh, is as sinful and bound to my lesser self as the next person. I can therefore write on the experience of peace, joy, and freedom due only to an amazing grace that saved my soul and a Spirit who guides and empowers my actions, made available to me by my just, merciful, and loving heavenly Father.

It is *only* through His love that I have any hope of conquering the lesser version of myself that is characterized by the constant opponents (like insecurity, selfishness, doubt, fear, and regret, to name a few) of my becoming the me I was created to be. While I don't mention any of the above to alienate, judge, or condemn anyone, this work will be undoubtedly influenced by my faith; I want to be forthcoming about that. In fact, its title comes from a passage of Scripture found in Romans 8:31–32, 37–39, which says:

> If God is for us, who can be against us? He who did not spare his own Son, but gave him up for us all—how will he not also, along with him, graciously give us all things? . . . In all these things we are more than conquerors through him who loved us. For I'm convinced that [nothing] will be able to separate us from the love of God that is in Christ Jesus our Lord.

This verse reminds me that God is for me, not against me. He also loves me, despite my weakness, and desires for me to share an eternal communion with Him—so much so that He sent His Son, Jesus, to pay the price for my sins so that I can be received as flawless in the presence of a holy, just, and perfect God. The best news ever is that the same is true for you! Now, with appropriate credit, gratitude, and glory being given to whom it is due, let's dive in.

KEEPING IT SIMPLE

I was in Chapel Hill, North Carolina, in the spring of 2024 when the legendary college football coach Mack Brown said the following to his team after an on-field fight between two of his players during a spring practice: "Men, there's little room for undisciplined actions if being a champion is your goal. The difference between winning and losing always ends up coming down to a handful of moments. Guys, *football is a simple game, but it's hard to play*, and we make it harder when we lack self-discipline."

The reason his statement resonated with me, twenty-plus years removed from wearing a helmet and shoulder pads as a walk-on quarterback at Michigan State University, was that it summarized a key point in this book. *Life* is also a simple game, but it's not easy to play, and our only chance to live *from* the victory that has been won for us is not from our own limited strength but with the power, love, and self-discipline that can be realized only through the indwelling of God's Holy Spirit. (See 2 Timothy 1:7.)

The self-improvement industry today is a global, multi-billion-dollar machine that largely fails to understand or convey this cornerstone truth. The size and impact of this industry, nonetheless, still serves as compelling evidence that we humans are starving to find a better way and a truth that will satisfy our souls' deep longings for fulfillment. At the same time, not only are the worldly instructions we receive flawed, but we're also distracted by work to complete, reputations to uphold, . . . and the list goes on.

All of these pursuits can easily lead us to chase endlessly after the wind, remaining in the unfulfilled condition that leaves us exhausted, frustrated, and empty. In the struggle we wonder whether this chase is all there is to know in life. Is the point of it all to go to school, find a job, jump into a lane, get married, have kids, own some stuff, live as prisoners of comparison, pay some bills, feel some thrills, and die?

While there are countless podcasts, YouTube channels, TED Talks, and books packed with unending content aimed at helping us "win in life," I have personally found that the only place where we can find these answers is in communion with the One who wrote the plan. Furthermore, my "winning" in this life will largely be based upon the quality of my character and the thoughts that I allow to direct my attitude and mindset.

Truth is, without a rock-solid identity and a courageous mentality (born only of an eternally unchanging and constant source), it is impossible to conquer what stands in the way of our realizing our full potential. Therefore, if victory is our goal, we can't live on the fleeting fortune-cookie wisdom of "following our hearts" and feelings. Instead, we need to train ourselves to receive the wisdom that guides our actions above our natural selves, in a productive and impactful manner, to experience God's best for us.

What are some obstacles that derail us in pursuit of a better way? Research done by *Harvard Business Review* and *Time* Magazine suggests:

Comfort zone, fear of failure, and giving up
Spiritual unawareness and lack of inner work (self-care)
Broken definitions of success and the approval of others

Wrong environment, shortsighted advice, vanity and pride
Self-limiting beliefs and limited confidence

Can you relate to any of these potential-limiting derailers? Has falling into these pitfalls led you to settle for less? I know I have. Fact is, we all have. Therefore, for those humble and hungry enough to listen, I share a way to build a simple bridge over life's unpredictable waters.

BRIDGE BUILDING

I personally began collecting thoughts for this book when the oldest of my three children was in middle school. I was checking in on her during the evening and noticed something different about her. The girl I had always known to be light-hearted and imaginative was noticeably down and deflated. For those who are reading this as parents, it is in these moments that we learn that the only thing tougher than dealing with challenges in our own lives is watching our children engage in theirs, without the sufficient life experiences or resources to address them effectively.

I suppose this is where next-level parenting begins. To make a long story short, she shared with me that evening that she had been on the receiving end of some "mean girl" criticism in school that day that she couldn't get out of her head. So, equipped with nothing more than my own life experiences and God's biblical truth to call upon, I began to do my parental best to reassure her that her identity and value as a person are in no way connected to the opinions of others. They are found in her being a child of the One true loving and eternal God who made her wonderfully and with perfect intent: nothing less and nothing more.

We talked about how possessing this foundational sense of value and identity is required for us to live life with the fearless mentality and the humble confidence our loving heavenly Father calls us to. Once our talk concluded, she gave me a big hug and thanked me for the advice. The next evening I could see that the light had returned to her eyes, and she declared that she'd had a great day at school because of her ongoing recollection of our talk and her continual adjusting of her perspective according to it. In that moment I knew I needed to recapture the high points of that Identity and Mentality conversation. As time went on, I began to intentionally emphasize these same critical truths to my younger two children, as well as to anyone else whom I felt could benefit from the difference-making encouragement in similar moments.

There was even a distinct moment in time when I had a vision of offering this important message, rooted in the life-giving gospel of Jesus Christ that He shared and modeled on this same earth over two thousand years ago, impacting so many lives with His truth through it. So, after receiving this vision, I decided it was time to started converting my "talk notes" into a book.

Ultimately, I wanted to build a bridge for others (my kids, first and foremost) by setting forth some basic life expectations and pointing toward a simple wisdom that helps us grow through life's challenges. I also wanted to share the belief that all we experience in this life is designed to add to our fulfillment and prepare us to live out our God-given purpose to our fullest potential.

As time went on, future talks with my younger son and daughter (in addition to conversations with others from all ages, genders, and backgrounds I've had the privilege to coach through the years) would add key themes to the Identity and Mentality foundation of this simple message. It is the culmination of these points, revealed through my experiencing this life and coaching others with those lessons learned, that led to the writing of this book.

You will find that most chapters offer relevant Scripture passages and poems to reinforce key content. I'll begin that routine here by sharing a poem titled "The Bridge Builder" by Will Allen Dromgoole, as a great articulation of my intent for writing this book.

An old man going a lone highway,
Came, at the evening cold and gray,
To a chasm vast and deep and wide.
Through which was flowing a sullen tide
The old man crossed the twilight dim,
The sullen stream had no fear for him;
But he turned when safe on the other side
And built a bridge to span the tide.
"Old man," said a fellow pilgrim near,
"You are wasting your strength with building here;
Your journey will end with the ending day,
You never again will pass this way;
You've crossed the chasm, deep and wide,
Why build this bridge at evening tide?"
The builder lifted his old gray head;
"Good friend, in the path I have come," he said,
"There followed me today
A youth whose feet must pass this way,
This chasm that has been as naught to me
To that fair-haired youth may a pitfall be;
He, too, must cross in twilight dim;
Good friend, I am building this bridge for him!"

Are you interested in effectively crossing life's turbulent waters, while becoming the conqueror your Creator designed you to be? As you consider this question, I want you to know that, while the "front door" of this book may appeal primarily to young men, given my personal experiences and background as the messenger, there is plenty of room for anyone interested to enter and participate in this journey that I share from my authentic individual perspective.

Regardless of our current situations or backgrounds, I have learned that, while God put us on this earth to experience His presence and do good, we have an enemy who never stops in his effort to steal from us and bring us harm. Oftentimes he will use our uncertainties and insecurities to hold us back so that he can do just that!

When we examine life in its simplest form, it is important for us to *know* that the Author of goodness (God) wants us to experience a full and abundant life, while the author of evil (the devil) wants to enslave us (John 10:10). But thanks be to God, it is in that very opposition that His Good News is found! God loves you so much that He made a way for you to conquer your evil enemy and live life in union with Him! He did this by sharing the Way to eternal peace and joy in His Word, showing the Way through His Son (Jesus), and powering the Way for all who believe through His Holy Spirit. His love is constant, unchanging, and full of truth and grace—and it is the place where our victory is found. So, if you're ready to live life from His victory, trading your emptiness for His fulfillment in accordance with the Conqueror's Way, . . . let's go!

INTRODUCTION

PERSONAL BACKGROUND

THE WONDER YEARS

While I don't consider my story to be extraordinary, it is my story, nonetheless, and it has played a role in shaping the man I've become. With that in mind I will share in this chapter a summary of my significant early life experiences to provide insight into the people, places, and events that have influenced and shaped me.

I was born the youngest of three kids into an ordinary, middle-class, suburban home and raised by my loving parents, Jerry and Phyllis Barkey in Warren, Michigan. My sister, Lori, is twelve years my elder, and my brother, Steve, was born ten years prior to me. As a kid I loved (and still do love) my big sis and bro. Lori was always protective of me and accompanied me on adventures. I looked up to Steve, and he inspired many of my life's early interests. Once Lori and Steve had moved out (Lori got married, and Steve went to college), it was just my parents and me.

My dad was a career General Motors man. In addition to working at GM's global headquarters in Warren, Michigan, he also loved woodworking. When he wasn't using his hands, he was using his voice and other musical gifts to participate in our church orchestra and choir and even singing bass in a gospel quartet. My mom, also a gifted musician (pianist), was our church secretary and had a passion for all things tea.

I am beyond grateful that God gave me Jerry and Phyllis as parents. My gratitude stems from the fact that they chose to point me, at a young age, toward God. While they weren't perfect (none of us are), my dad was consistent and set the example for how a leader guides, provides for, and prioritizes family before self, and Mom was a tender-hearted and thoughtful companion to him in that work. As a result, my upbringing provided me with love and an opportunity to pursue my interests. So, what did those early pursuits look like?

From my earliest days those interests were tied to sports. My first love in sport was baseball. I have many memories of my dad helping to coach my Little League teams, playing catch with me in the backyard, and taking me to Tiger games.

It was also in 1984 that my brother, Steve, introduced me to football. I remember the first Super Bowl I ever watched: Super Bowl XIX—Joe Montana's San Francisco 49ers defeated Dan Marino's Miami Dolphins. Technically, this was the *first second half* of a Super Bowl I ever watched—my parents were uncompromising on the fact that we would be in church *every* Sunday night while I was growing up. I have other memories of my big brother taking me into the backyard to walk me through his JV football passing plays. I loved spending that time with him.

Being involved in church was also a big piece of my growing up experience. While my faith and understanding of God and His plan for me have grown throughout my life, Warren Woods Church of the Nazarene was where the seeds of God's truth were planted in my life. It was also through this church that I made friends and was offered my first job by my pastor, Jim Mellish. He was a great guy (a sports-lover, too) who trusted me as an early teen with the responsibility of mowing our church's (and church school's) grass. It was a big deal to me to learn both to ride and to maintain the big John Deere tractor-mower!

COLLEGE AND CAREER

As I grew into my high school years, sports were to play a role in both the way I was perceived by others and how I viewed myself. Being voted captain on my varsity football and baseball teams by my teammates were both meaningful honors to me at that time. Eventually, I earned a scholarship to play football and baseball at NAIA Olivet Nazarene University in Kankakee, Illinois.

After attending Olivet Nazarene during my freshman fall semester, I was encouraged by my brother to share some of my freshman practice film with Michigan State's football program. While I didn't expect that anything would come of it, I responded to his nudge and did just that. Two days later I received a phone call while I was home for Christmas break. "Jeremy, Coach Saban and I just watched your tape, and I would like to offer you a roster spot as a preferred walk-on quarterback." The person making that call was the MSU football offensive coordinator Gary Tranquill and I accepted his offer.

While I never made it on to the game field for the Spartans, this experience opened the door to many opportunities for me. In addition to the lifelong friendships that were established, playing Big Ten football gave me the chance to do something I loved to do, daily, at a high level and for some great coaches. While playing quarterback at Michigan State, I was also able to play a pivotal role as a student athlete in implementing a chapter of

Athletes in Action (an on-campus fellowship for student athletes pursuing Christ).

In addition to my AIA involvement, I learned the inner workings of major college athletics after being selected by my coaches to serve as the football program's representative on the student Athlete Advisory Committee. It was also at MSU that I decided to pursue a career in education so that I could apply a lifelong passion for teaching and coaching.

As great as these experiences were, however, the most significant thing that happened to me during those years was reconnecting with my high school sweetheart, Samantha. Soon after graduating, Samantha and I were engaged and bought our first home. I also accepted my first career teaching and coaching job in Colorado, where we would spend the first two years of our married lives together until she became pregnant with our first child, Isabella.

We eventually moved back to Michigan, and over the course of the next seven years I would continue to work as a high school teacher and coach, while Samantha and I rounded out our family of five with the addition of two more kids, Landon and Ellie.

During those years I grew as a person, teacher, and coach. While I coached several different sports, coaching football was what I enjoyed most, and I did that until I decided to pursue advancement in the education career I had chosen. At the age of thirty-two I became a high school athletic director and would hold that post at two different schools over the next five years. It was during that five-year span that challenges I encountered, both personally and professionally, led me to lean more deeply into a relationship with God through Jesus Christ, as God used trials to strengthen and mold me.

RAILROAD METAPHOR

Before we get started with exploring our simple framework, I'm going to take a moment to introduce a metaphor I will be using to further support central themes in *The Conqueror's Way*. The visual learner in me always appreciates a good metaphor to enhance my understanding of important material, so I forward that benefit to you as well. Our metaphor will specifically compare the application of our framework to the construction of a railroad track designed to transport people and goods to a specific destination. We'll also examine the assembly of a coal-fired locomotive engine that would ride the rails. I have found this imagery to provide a fitting visual to run alongside the Conqueror's Way, which emphasizes forward movement, regardless of circumstance, in pursuit of a purposeful destination—that of realizing our dreams and reaching our fullest God-given potential. Metaphoric summaries will be provided at the end of each chapter to highlight key themes.

CHAPTER 1

THE CONQUEROR'S IDENTITY

Mirror of Truth

"It never ceases to amaze me: we all love ourselves more than other people but care more about their opinion than our own."

MARCUS AURELIUS

Who am I? For each one of us there are layers to that answer. Regardless of your response to that question, what is true for all of us is that the way we see ourselves has a tremendous impact on how we live our lives. Should that perception be based on our successes and failures, the applause or criticism we have received, the statuses we have attained, or what other people say about us? How often do our pursuits (or avoidance of worthy pursuits) stem primarily from a desire to be accepted by others?

Is it possible that our identity is not about any of this? Could our individuality and value be more about from where, and whom, we have come? Could the pivot point for us be a reliable source of unconditional love and the sense of belonging all humans need? How different might your life look if your concept of self were rooted in your being the recipient of an unfailing love offered by an unchanging, just, and merciful God who sees you as His child—a perception in no way affected by your failures, painful memories, and shortcomings? Would you feel differently about yourself? Your intrinsic value? Your worth? How might this affect your life's foundation?

According to Webster's dictionary, one's identity has to do with the character of that individual. Webster also alludes that it is sameness (or oneness or consistency or predictability) that constitutes the objective reality of any person or thing. We can summarize Webster's two points on identity by saying that (1) our personal identity is defined by our character and that (2) it is what we consistently do, not merely say, that establishes that character.

When it comes to establishing our identity and our character, whose standard and example are we reaching for? Is this a standard worth pursuing? What if we fall? Furthermore, how do we go about creating a healthy sameness (a consistent, reliable self) from which to live our lives, given our imperfections? Your answers to these questions will serve as the cornerstone of your existence. Answers that point to a firm foundation of unfailing, unconditional, and constant love will reflect a self-image that allows you to boldly pursue great challenges. Conversely, answering those questions in a way that neglects this human need reveals an unstable foundation that will ensure only disappointment, frustration, and spiritual devastation when life's storms hit.

NOT MEASURING UP

I learned this lesson after moving on from high school teaching and coaching to securing what I thought would be my forever dream job as a high school athletic director. Those expectations were disrupted when, a year and a half into this opportunity, I found myself failing in that role due to personal leadership missteps rooted in insecurity and arrogance. It was during this season that I, for the first time in my life, was forced to deal with significant disappointment, frustration, and shame. After having been approached by my superiors at that time with the news that this situation was not working out the way they had hoped when I was hired, I found myself dealing with a sense of brokenness and embarrassment I had never known before.

Who am I? I wondered. If I were what my job title claimed me to be, a high school athletic director, I must not have been a very good one. It was during this time that God mercifully taught me that who I was had nothing to do with my personal successes or failures or with the acceptance, praise, and approval of others. He taught me this lesson by providing a blessed assurance for my soul that His unfailing and unconditional love for me would never change.

Most importantly, this truth had nothing to do with my performance but everything to do with His character. In an undeniable way, He met me in my despair and assured me that His plan for my life could still be realized despite my current circumstances. At that moment, realizing that this pursuit (while well intentioned) had been all about my efforts to add value and worth to my own existence, I decided to release control of my fleshly ambition, repent of my human error, and recenter my life on this firm foundation as I sought His will for my future. From that point on I would be only who God said I was, a loved child of His.

JUST AS I AM

Have you ever felt that way? As if your worth as a human being were tied to your accomplishments or reputation. Have you found yourself standing on this shaky foundation, uncertain of your identity in those moments? This type of traumatic life event can either make or break some people and can have a tremendous impact on the overall trajectory of their lives.

When we have a rock-solid identity, built on our Creator's unchanging, unfailing, and unconditional love and valuation instead of on the fleeting opinions of others, that trajectory changes for the better. On the other hand, if we allow these temporary circumstances to warp our perception of self, we can experience a demoralizing downward spiral as a result. The reality is that every human being has an inherent need for love and belonging. If we seek these qualities in unstable sources, we will never know peace in, or have a firm foundation for, our lives. Isaiah 43:1–2, which has become one of my favorite Scripture passages, provides a written reminder of the stability and unchanging nature of the love that God alone provides:

> "Do not fear, for I have redeemed you;
> I have summoned you by name; *you are mine.*
> When you pass through the waters,
> I will be with you;
> And when you pass through the rivers,
> they will not sweep over you.
> When you walk through the fire,
> you will not be burned." (emphasis added)

The truth is that we all need this assurance for life's trying times. That passage from Isaiah serves as a much-needed reminder that the eternal and loving God of all creation *chose* you and me and that we both belong and matter to Him! You are not a cosmic accident, just passing through this existence by random chance, left alone to live as a slave to your insecurities and dependent on the fulfillment of your fleshly desires. You were created not only with careful intent but in that Creator's very image.

ROCK OF CONSTANCY

Let's take a quick moment to restate this truth in practical terms. When we are in school, we learn about Sir Isaac Newton's Third Law of Motion, which informs us that movement of any kind results from outside action and force. We know, consequently, that the force required to initiate and sustain the very breath in our lungs and the beating of our hearts comes from beyond us. Right? Why is it, then, that, while we understand this physical reality, it can take painful life events for us to come to know, and *believe*, that this same all-powerful force (God) who initiates and sustains the physical life of every living being on this planet also cares deeply about our emotional well-being (regardless of our striving) and wants us to know that He desires to live in *relationship* with us, both in this life and throughout eternity?

The sooner we embrace this reality, the better off we'll be. After all, it is only through a relationship with the Creator of the universe (who is also our personal Savior and Sustainer) that healthy relationship with other humans is possible. Without it we experience life as a rollercoaster ride of insecurity that places unfair expectations on others to meet needs that only God can meet, which in turn creates unfair animus against others and instability within ourselves.

For me personally, before *experiencing* His mercy I was driven by a misguided belief that actions aligned with religious guidelines earned me God's acceptance and approval. While I had always believed, thanks to my upbringing, that my eternal salvation has been secured through Jesus's death and resurrection, I hadn't personally received His unconditional Father love for me until this event; it was here and then that He met me, beneath the crushing weight of my failure. Whether through personal or professional challenges in my adult life since, God has mercifully reminded me again and again that His love is constant and unchanging, even when I fail or can't feel His presence. This is so much different from what we learn through human relationship, where our errors and shortcomings are sure to create frustration in others.

Have you ever lived in this new and invigorating way? Are you living this way now? The main problem with allowing our identity and ego to be built on achievement, praise, and popularity (even though it feels great when things are going well) is that when we encounter the opposite (criticism, defeat, and rejection) we experience the fragility of what we've built. We all need unconditional love that is constant and unlimited. When we realize that we already have this in the God of the universe who created us, we see ourselves as we truly are: *chosen*, valued, and infinitely loved . . . no matter what.

In doing research for this book, I learned, through a conversation with the Michigan State Psychology professor Dr. Lonny Rosen (who also helped Coach Saban establish "the Process" during our 1998 MSU football season), that the psychology community has validated the importance of an individual's developing a certainty of unchanging and constant love in their lives, even when that source is unseen. This psychological theory is called *object constancy*, and those who have it in their lives experience a more fulfilled and stable existence than those who don't. An added benefit of object constancy is emotional permanence, which allows us to trust that our deepest needs are cared for, freeing us to effectively relate with, love, and trust others.

Are these dots connecting? Can you see why having a relationship with (not a religious observance of) God, the One constant rock we can depend on in a world of continuous and chaotic change, is so critical? Without a sense of loving object constancy with our Maker, we'll always lack the emotional permanence required for maintaining balance in life. Even worse, lacking emotional permanence leads us to people-pleasing behaviors, in the hope of garnering the unfailing love and acceptance we need from sources that aren't qualified or able to give it. This is why Jesus pointed anyone who would listen back to Himself as the only source of foundational and constant truth. We see this in Matthew 7:24–27:

> "Therefore, everyone who hears these words of mine and puts them into practice is like a wise man who built his house on the rock. The rain came down, the streams rose, and the winds blew and beat against that house; yet it did not fall, because it had its foundation on the rock. But everyone who hears these words of mine and does not put them into practice is like a foolish man who built his house on sand. The rain came down, the streams rose, and the winds blew and beat against that house, and it fell with a crash."

For me, it was getting rejected by those whose approval I sought that led me to recognize the sandy, shifting foundation on which I was building my life. It led me to earnestly explore *who, and whose,* I am. Thanks to God's mercy, He answered both of those basic questions and got my feet back on solid ground. It took one undeniable moment of acknowledgment for me to feel His love and acceptance that were bringing me back to the firmest possible foundation so I could move forward. As a result, I made a commitment to myself and to my God to build a relationship with Him and to live only for the approval of an audience of One (God), whose unfailing love remains constant and unchanging, regardless of my circumstances.

A FATHER'S CHARACTER

Think for a moment about your history of relationships. Have you ever been close to someone you didn't know or spend time with? Of course not. It's no different with God. If we want a real relationship with Him, we must not only pursue Him but get to know Him and understand His character. God is far more interested in a relationship with us than He ever was in our observance of a religion that adopts His name. When we come to a place where we genuinely want to spend time with God to understand more of who He is (His character attributes and standards), this is where life change begins.

As I began to study God's Word more deeply and intently following that difficult season brought on by my professional failure, I was quick to identify and experience the character attributes of God that I had learned about through Scripture when I was younger. Attributes expressed in adjectives like *holy, loving, just, merciful, gracious,* and *wise*. This time through, however, it became clear to me that God intended for *me* to be identified by *His* character attributes, so that I could reflect His name(s), image, and likeness (The Ultimate NIL deal) and thereby share His light and love with the world around me, in His name.

When studying the various names of God in Scripture—such as the Great "I AM," the "Mighty Creator," and the "Healer"—I was overwhelmed with exultant thoughts of His wonder and goodness. My soul, however, felt more inclined to respond to other names like the "Faithful Father," "the LORD who Provides," and the "Defender" and "Protector." I suppose this inclination had something to do with the awesome responsibility I was feeling as a parent for my kids (to faithfully provide for, defend, and protect them). If you are a parent, you may feel similarly compelled.

While God is certainly aware of the limitations of His human creations, He calls us to relationship with Himself, so that we can learn what it means to live out our responsibilities as He intended, and as He demonstrated—to exemplify all His character attributes and names, as found in biblical Scripture. Once our knowledge of His expectations, standards, and example is met with an authentic spiritual and emotional experience of His Fatherly love, we are ready to pursue His will for us from a place of love, rather than because of religious obligation.

Before I understood this, I lived in denial that I, a person raised in a Christian church, lived with the same human condition and flaws as the next person; I didn't really need the love of my heavenly Father, I reasoned, if I didn't do the bad things that would stoke His anger. Crazy, right? The reality is that we all need to experience His immutable Fatherly love; if we don't, we will aim to find a substitute, either consciously or unconsciously, elsewhere. This creates all kinds of issues for us as humans. When we go through life not having the blessed assurance that we are enough—not because of how good we are but because of how great God is—we will always question whether our best is sufficient.

Perhaps you've found (or find) yourself in a similar circumstance, dealing with the frustration of a failure and the confusing emotions that follow; if so, you can relate to my story, even if you haven't been able to make sense of your own yet. Maybe you can relate to not really knowing *who*, or *whose*, you are. Or possibly you realize that you are held hostage by your insecurities and are tired of acting *from* this force in your life rather than functioning *above* it.

Whatever the case, I want you to know that your heavenly Father is for you, not against you, and that He wants to set you on a path that leads to experiencing His love so you can realize your potential. Furthermore, His love is a gift He wants you to receive. When you receive His gift and repent of (turn away from) the selfish motives that undermine your existence, your life will never again be the same.

So, what does putting our best foot forward look like after receiving this gift? In his book titled *Identity*, T. D. Jakes declares, "As long as you strive to be someone you're not, you will never fulfill your purpose." I agree. Have you ever invested in time and effort-wasting pursuits that were more about your ego craving the approval of others than about applying the *real* you toward your life's work? We simply can't "win" as anyone else in life, no matter what outside influences may suggest to us. Living in society today is not easy. With social media, many are constantly leveraging likes, hearts, and follows to shape what we want the world to see of us, based on how our insecurities would like us to be seen. And for what? Do we truly believe other people care that much?

Have you ever struggled with "less than" thoughts? Bought into self-limiting beliefs? Talked negatively to yourself about yourself? Doubted yourself? Felt as if you weren't enough? Your only legitimate counter truth to those lies is the fact that God made you in His own image and has worked out a way for you to reflect Him and all the traits that comprise His character. Hearts, likes, and follows can't hold a candle to that.

We weren't created to please everyone we encounter in our lives. Furthermore, when we truly live for the One who loved us first, His light creates enough self-awareness to expose our imperfection and limitations, . . . and that's okay. Once He reveals these areas to us, however, it is up to us to take steps to do something about them if we are serious about living as the best possible versions of ourselves.

After discovering that our sense of acceptance and approval shouldn't come from others, we need to be able to gauge our integrity. This requires the work of establishing our core beliefs (built on values) that allow us to stand upright in a world of competing pressures and priorities. Once we crystallize these beliefs, we need to live a life of integrity that demonstrates an alignment between those beliefs (or values) and our daily behaviors. Being individuals of integrity and staying true to ourselves is the *only way* to experience God's best for us.

While I've always carried a notion of what integrity is, it wasn't until I had truly grasped this simple definition (value and behavior alignment) that I was truly able to live in pursuit of it. An aspiration of righteousness or extraordinary morality was just too comprehensive for me to attain in my flesh. The outcome always reverted to my trying to present in a manner worthy of praise to others, as opposed to doing the hard work of assessing my values and discerning God's will for me. If this were going to be different moving forward, I would need to create and own an easy-to-use measurement with which to assess whether I was on track in my pursuit of God's best for me.

It was with that realization that I decided to establish my personal core values. By that I mean to highlight the nonnegotiable core beliefs that would embody what I stand for and influence the choices I would make. After taking time to assess what mattered most to me in life, and in consideration of the character bar set and modeled for me by my audience of One (God), I eventually settled on the three nonnegotiable core values of Growth, Purpose, and Solidarity. I believed that, if I were to consistently adhere to this value compass, I could experience the peace, joy, and freedom I desired.

The value of Growth states that I want to be a person who pursues challenges while trying to realize my fullest potential. I don't want to be a person who gravitates toward the comfortable spaces that would keep me from discovering what God intends for me. The value of Purpose states that I have been created intentionally and purposefully by a loving God to whom I belong and who wants me to pursue Him with my whole heart.

Everyone's purpose is tied to serving others in some way. Purpose is one of God's laws of nature that is evident in everything we see, from the trees that provide our oxygen to the sun that perfectly heats and brings balance to our solar system. When we serve others by using our gifts, we glorify the God who gave us those gifts in the first place.

Finally, the value of Solidarity articulates for me that I want to be a person who is faithful to my purpose, my God, and the people to whom I have committed. It also reminds me to be selective about the people I associate with, given the fact that my ability to live out the first two values will be largely influenced by my inner circle. If my behaviors are misaligned with these beliefs (which has certainly happened in my life), I will know where correction was needed—not based on the opinions of others but on honest reflection.

At the end of the day, this last value is where integrity comes from, and it has the greatest impact on our self-confidence. No matter how undetectable to the people around us, the deepest parts of our being know when our values and behaviors are in conflict. Consider what it feels like to be "off" or "on" as you live through the ebb and flow of life. When you reflect on the "off" times, I'd be willing to bet that your core beliefs and daily actions were in misalignment. We cannot discover our best version and positively impact the world around us while lacking that alignment. This is why integrity matters.

Furthermore, if we don't live as people of integrity by creating *habits* that allow us to live as one integrated self and receive care from our heavenly Father, we will fall back into seeking our identity in the things that bring us momentary gratification and garner the approval of others. I find myself moved by a great poem on the theme of integrity, "Man in the Glass," written by Peter Dale Wimbrow in 1934:

> When you get what you want in your struggle for self
> And the world makes you king for a day,
> Just take a quick moment, go grab a mirror,
> And see what that man has to say.
> For it isn't a man's father, mother, or wife
> Whose judgement upon him must pass.
> The fellow whose verdict counts most in his life,
> Is the one staring back from the glass.

He's the fellow to please, never mind all the rest,
Because he's with you clear till the end.
And you've passed your most dangerous and difficult test
If the man in the glass is your friend.
You can fool the whole world down the pathway of years
and get pats on the back as you pass
But your final reward will be heartache and tears,
If you've cheated the man in the glass.

Have you cheated yourself by allowing someone else's opinion of you to be the basis for your sense of self-worth or identity? If so, you're not alone. I would even argue that we live today amid a global identity crisis—which is exactly what our enemy wants. Keep your eyes off God's simple truth (that *He is for us* and values us so highly that He sent His Son to make a Way for us), grow your insecurity, obsess over what other people think, . . . and then watch the exhausting and life-stealing scramble ensue.

When we are awakened to this reality, it's up to us to do something about it. So, where is it that we do the work of considering whether our daily behaviors align with our values? You need a space to set aside for this work, a space apart from distractions. The truest form of self-care is to create a *habit* that dedicates time and space to the important work of repetition and routine. To go through the thoughtful exercise of establishing your values and character goals so that you can live with integrity, as "one self"—but then to fail to prioritize the time necessary to create the habits that support that pursuit—is like finishing a work of art and then setting it in the middle of a road to be shredded by life's incessant traffic.

Personally, as I moved forward beyond my failure, I decided that I was finished seeing myself as any less than God, who sent His perfect Son Jesus Christ to pay the price for my sin and imperfection, does. When I looked into the mirror, I realized that God created, loved, and equipped me (despite my limitations) for whatever it was he had me on this earth to do.

There is a biblical proverb that observes, "As a man 'thinketh in his heart, so is he'" (Proverbs 23:7 KJV). I have found this to be true. Until we see ourselves as children of God, approved of and loved by the Creator of this universe, we will always feel defeated by our failures, fall back into our insecurities, and avoid pursuits that can reveal God's intention for us.

Have you ever shied away from pursuing an opportunity that you felt could have brought you closer to your destiny? Was insecurity or a "less than" view of yourself the cause? As God's children, we are royalty heirs who have been given more than enough to live in pursuit of His best. Protecting this sense of identity with healthy habits that reflect this belief is key. Without them you'll struggle to maintain the authentic integrity needed for you to thrive in your pursuit.

HABIT FORMATION

With that in mind, I invite you to commit to pursuing *consistency* over perfection as you develop new habits. As you're being truthful with yourself about those character flaws that need addressing, give yourself a fair measure of grace. Our best is all we can give, so commit to giving this path your best effort and rolling with the punches along the way. Prioritize and adjust, and you *will* see results over time. As you reflect on your journey, where it has brought you and where it seems to be taking you, don't assume that the same skills and traits that brought you this far will be the ones to lead you further. While as a child of God you are certainly equipped to be successful in the opportunities that lie ahead, your traits need to be developed and refined, and new skills need to be adopted, if progressing effectively through your life's journey is your goal.

For starters, you'll need to commit to regularly caring for your own intellectual, physical, emotional, and spiritual well-being. This includes getting to know God by seeking Him *first*, without distraction, at the start of every day. To do this well you'll need to wake up early every morning to spend time in quiet solitude with your audience of One. It is during this time that you can both bring your requests to Him and listen for His direction.

If personal growth and living out your God-given identity really matter to you, coasting along and getting by on being a likable person who goes through life without intentionally applying whatever talents you've been given won't work. Furthermore, if you find yourself in an employment position that requires you to serve and lead others effectively, you'll need to rest and recalibrate daily. Establishing a morning routine that begins with God is the best way to get started. Next, you'll need to do the honest and intentional work of establishing your core values and then prioritize the best focus time (perhaps built into your new morning routine) to determine whether your daily actions are aligning with your core values.

Finally, the most significant habit you can establish is daily Bible reading. By engaging with the Bible regularly you will become more familiar with God's unchanging character and heart toward you. You can start small here and eventually, over time, begin to commit Scripture verses to memory for easy recall of truth when life throws its unexpected curveballs that have the potential to disrupt your path. If you want to live a life rooted in truth, you must get familiar with its source. The apostle Paul's words in Ephesians 6:10–17 provide a great framework for practicing the habits that can keep our feet on a firm foundation:

> Finally, be strong in the Lord and in his mighty power . . . so that you can take your stand against the devil's schemes . . . Put on the full armor of God, so that when the day of evil comes, you may be able to stand your ground . . . Stand firm then, with the belt of truth buckled around your waist, with the breastplate of righteousness in place, and with your feet fitted with the readiness that comes from the gospel of peace. In addition . . ., take up the shield of faith, with which you can extinguish all the flaming arrows of the evil one. Take the helmet of salvation and the sword of the Spirit, which is the word of God.

We know that our enemy does not mean well for us. His attacks focus on the very core of your identity: your heart. He knows that, if he can successfully distract you from these simple, yet profound daily habits, he can play on your insecurities and uncertainties to drive you away from building a meaningful relationship with God, who is the only One who is able to provide the firm foundation of love and peace that you need if you desire to live effectively, according to your Maker's design. A thirty-minute dose of biblical Scripture at a Sunday church service can't be your only source of weekly truth—not if proactively protecting your heart is the goal. We need Him and His truth every second of every minute of every hour of every day!

Notice in the Ephesians passage that Paul references the Word as the sword of the Spirit. Note further that it is the only offensive weapon referenced in the "armor of God" passage. Without our reliance upon it, the limitations of our human knowledge will fail us, and the enemy's schemes will defeat us.

The habits of reflecting on and reading the Word that He provides equip us with His protection so we can stay alert and ready to take the fight to the enemy when he attacks. Pursuing God's character and committing to habits that support this pursuit make it possible to consistently act justly, love mercy, and walk humbly with God as believers are called to do.

Railroad Metaphor: Firm Foundation

In this chapter we learned that our sense of Identity is the foundation of our lives. Just as the foundation of a railroad track, called ballast, consists of rock, our life's foundation should be comprised of the unchanging and rock-solid truth of God—and that includes accepting and internalizing what He says about us. Furthermore, embedded into the ballast are sleepers, the wooden planks to which the rails are affixed. Sleepers are one with the ballast and play a critical role in providing a balanced support system. Without sleepers the rails would rest on the ballast unsecured, rendering them prone to sinking and unable to support forward movement.

In our metaphor the sleepers are akin to Jesus Christ, who is joined to God the Father. Establishing an object-constant, rock-solid relationship with God through Jesus creates a firm and reliable surface for our life's tracks. If that relationship is strong, our tracks can move us forward and take us far. If this foundation is either absent or compromised, however, we will be easily mired in shifting terrain.

IDENTITY TAKEAWAY . . .

God's Provision and Protection are your Salvation and Shield!

You are a child of God, wonderfully designed with the capacity to demonstrate all of your heavenly Father's traits. Furthermore, God created you for a specific purpose, chose you, and paid the highest price for you because of His unchanging love for you. As His child, you belong to your loving heavenly Father and Savior, no matter what happens in your life! By His mercy, He wants you to live in intimate relationship with Him, on a firm foundation of truth and justice that keeps you on your feet and protects you from the enemy of your soul.

QUESTIONS: Do you know this love today? How might living from a foundation of this provision and protection from your heavenly Father change your life?

APPLICATION: Take time to establish your values as a person. These values should represent the standard you desire to resemble and should be nonnegotiable in nature. Once you've done this, establish a routine that allows you to reflect on your behavior's alignment to these values. *Take time* to learn God's truth through Scripture.

CHAPTER 2

THE CONQUEROR'S MENTALITY
Choosing Courage

"To be an overachiever, you have to be an overbeliever."
DABO SWINNEY

Once a person knows the truth of where they come from and who they are, with their feet firmly planted on the rock-solid foundation of constant and unfailing love in their lives, they no longer need to win the approval of others. As a result, they are no longer overwhelmed or threatened by the fear of failure. While doubt and fear will always find ways to present themselves to us humans, those who have found security and stability in a relationship with an unchanging God can choose to live in His truth and embrace who He says we are, in Him, regardless of performance outcome or the opinions of others.

Secure in this knowledge, we can take on challenges more confidently and recognize opportunities in obstacles as we pursue the realization of living out our best versions of ourselves. To override the tendencies of our lesser versions, we need to daily train our focus and learn to take negative thoughts captive, so that we may rule over our circumstances.

We learn from Webster's dictionary that the word *mentality* is defined as a mental capacity or mode (a way) of *thought*. Simply stated, a person's mentality determines their outlook and perspective on the world around them, which in turn influences how they choose to engage with it. Furthermore, to live with a *Conqueror's Mentality* is to overcome our doubts, self-limiting beliefs, and fear of failure in courageous pursuit of meaningful triumph and impact.

If we are to live with a conqueror's mentality, our thoughts must be of good quality, and the attitudes that result from them should arise from a predisposition for choosing gratitude. When our mindsets are positioned for growth rather than mere survival, we believe that anything is possible and consider what can be achieved through our victories rather than being consumed by what could be lost if we fall short.

Living with a conqueror's mentality brings a peace of mind that emboldens our belief, permitting us to accurately assess danger so that we can decide to move forward in life *courageously*. There is work to be done to condition our minds to focus clearly and consistently and to live with a sense of positivity and possibility. By learning how to control the *thoughts* we dwell on, we can improve our attitudes and elevate our mindsets.

CHASING A CHALLENGE

In my personal journey I learned many of these lessons in my pursuit of a new athletic director leadership opportunity following my first stint in such a role. Before stepping out in a new direction I had a decision to make. Would I return to the familiar comforts of being a classroom teacher and football coach, or would I attempt to pursue a different athletic directorship opportunity, in a new setting, where I could apply valuable lessons learned and more effectively accomplish the outcomes I had hoped for all along?

I decided to pursue a new athletic director opportunity, and it was one of the best decisions I have ever made. Not long after I was encouraged by the first district to look for alternate employment, an amazing opportunity became available two towns over from where my family lived. After running through the selection process in this new school in a larger and more prominent district, I was offered the new opportunity.

The next three years would be incredibly rewarding, as I was to experience much of what I had hoped for in my first pursuit. This was primarily due to two variables. First, this district and specific school were a far better fit for my personal strengths, disposition, and vision. Second, I was committed to applying lessons learned from prior failings to improve my overall effectiveness in the role. As a result, our coaches, student athletes, and community experienced a wonderful time of growth for our program and success for the specific teams that competed in it.

Ultimately it was this turnaround in effectiveness and impact that would lead to an unexpected job offer and the next step in my professional journey, which I'll discuss further at the end of this chapter. For now, though, I want to share what it is I credit most for the sudden and positive change in my experience, not just as a leader but as an individual.

The difference maker for me was the changed Mentality that resulted from a new sense of Identity, which was now rooted in the unconditional love of God. With my self-doubt conquered through the security I found in God's unfailing love, I was able to lead with a humility that allowed me to genuinely put the well-being of others first, . . . and the results spoke for themselves. This type of humility doesn't just arise by chance. It developed for me as the byproduct of intentional choices I made and actions I took that led to better results.

FOCUSING ATTENTION

The busyness and chaos of life don't make focusing easy. We all encounter various pressures that compete for our attention. Nonetheless, once we learn the impact of our thoughts on the quality of our lives, we can dedicate the time, energy, and effort necessary to learn how to control and redirect our thoughts (through daily habits that aid us in submitting them to the light of God's truth). Simply stated, when we focus on the right things our outlook is clearer, and we make better decisions. Would you like your thoughts, and the attitude and mindset that are their fruit, to guide your daily life so you can know peace instead of worry and fear? Me, too! So, how do we realize this change? Let's start by looking at the word *attention*.

> **Attention:** (a) The act or state of applying the mind to something. (b) A condition of readiness involving a selective narrowing or focusing of consciousness.

If we want our attention to be set on that which brings us clarity and peace, we must redirect our focus away from distraction, chaos, regret, and confusion. In his book *Brain Rules*, John Medina (founding director of the Brain Center for Applied Learning) calls out what he refers to as "the myth of multi-tasking." The reality in our fast-paced lives is that, if we want clarity, we won't get it on the commute to work. If we want to hear from God, this won't happen as we fight for oxygen on a treadmill at the gym. As Medina puts it, we need to create "Interruption-Free Zones" void of email, phone calls, and social media if we truly hope to focus our minds. The apostle Paul in Philippians 4:4–13 instructs us to look to God for clarity:

> Rejoice in the Lord always, I will say it again: Rejoice!
> . . . Do not be anxious about anything, but in every situation, by prayer and petition, with thanksgiving, present your requests to God. And the peace of God, which transcends all understanding, will guard your hearts and minds in Christ Jesus.
>
> Finally, brothers and sisters, whatever is true, whatever is noble, whatever is right, whatever is pure, whatever is lovely, whatever is admirable—if anything is excellent or praiseworthy—think about such things. Whatever you have learned or received or heard from me or seen in me—put it into *practice*. And the God of peace will be with you.
>
> . . . I have learned to be content whatever the circumstances. I know what it is to be in need, and I know what it is to have plenty. I have learned the secret of being content in any and every situation. . .. *I can do all this through him who gives me strength* (emphasis added).

This is one of my favorite passages of Scripture, and it is chockfull of points pertinent to where we should place our focused attention when seeking clarity, direction, and peace. First, in verse 4 we see that Paul enjoins us to *choose* to rejoice in the Lord. The position and importance of this direction cannot be overstated. This speaks to Paul's own (remember that he was imprisoned in Rome while he wrote) regular practice of praising God in all circumstances for all that He is and has done.

If you're having a difficult time choosing what to rejoice about, how about starting with the truth we discussed in the Identity chapter? The God of the universe, who created and sustains all life, knows you fully, chose you, and loves you deeply, just as you are! Recalling this truth daily in our lives is the beginning of conquering fear and living with peace of mind.

Next, Paul tells us not to worry. None of us needs look very far to see the toll of worry in our world today. Anxiety and depression centered on self-deprecation and perceived lack have robbed countless lives of peace. As a result, we have created an entire sector of the pharmaceutical industry aimed at attacking worry-driven anxiety through medicine. While I'm certainly not suggesting that medication for debilitating anxiety and depression are never appropriate, I am saying that I would never jump to those solutions without first leaning into uninterrupted meditation and prayer.

It has been said that worry is a conversation you have with yourself about things you cannot change, while prayer is a dialogue with God about things that only He can change. I have personally found this to be true. When we cast our cares on God through prayer and focus on His magnitude and greatness through meditation, our challenges shrink down to size. Problems that once seemed larger than life are cut down to a manageable size with fresh, godly perspective.

Have you ever found yourself lying awake at night wondering how a certain situation was going to play out? I know I have. In those moments I have learned to convert my worrisome monologue into a grateful dialogue with God. The results of this practice confirmed in my life Paul's prayer antidote to worry. In those two-way talks I experienced God's peace as I set my focus on Him and laid my limited understanding at His feet. It is in such moments that I can feel His presence with me, which immediately alters my perspective considering His greatness (converting challenges into opportunities instead of problems), giving me peace amid whatever circumstances I might be facing.

ATTITUDE OF GRATITUDE

Once we have learned how to direct our attention productively, we can shape a more consistently positive attitude. So, what exactly is attitude, anyway?

Attitude: A feeling or emotion toward a fact or state.

Our attitude, like our attention, is ours to determine. If it is shaped by positivity, optimism, which is the ability to consistently anticipate or visualize best possible outcomes, will influence our outlook. While it's true that an optimistic attitude does not guarantee best outcomes all the time, it is conversely true that negativity tends to *ensure* failure.

But can we really live consistently with optimistic attitudes in the turmoil, chaos, and uncertainty of our daily lives? My answer is yes, and I'll again point toward another simple biblical solution offered by Paul in Philippians 4. Both the quality of our thoughts and our ability to focus our attention positively shape our attitudes. In verse 6, where Paul tells us to bring our petitions to God in prayer, he calls us to thanksgiving as an antidote to anxiety.

Neuroscience tells us that the practice of gratitude in our lives brings many positive effects, including the release of dopamine and serotonin. These chemicals reset our brain's wiring; reduce stress; and improve our sleep, moods, and even our immunity. This is why choosing to be grateful in any circumstance is essential.

Each of us has blessings in our lives to be grateful for—we just need to pause to see them. Then we need to take inventory of our blessings. How? Through meditation and journaling. We list the blessings we are grateful for and meditate on the *Giver* of those gifts. When we do this our gratitude inventory serves as a neurological wall to defend against a feeling of being overwhelmed, discouragement, and the invasion of sad and anxious thoughts. Our meditation on the Gift-Giver provides a contented peace that alters our perspective.

I certainly understand that practicing all of this can be easier said than done, especially since the object of our focus (God) cannot be seen physically. It is through our mind's eye, however, that we can see Him and feel His presence in those still, meditative moments.

If you find yourself stuck in your efforts toward gratitude journaling or meditating on God, try adding music to your routine. It has been said that music is the language of the soul and that listening to music that offers praise and worship to the Creator and sustainer of your soul can be just what the doctor ordered to center your thoughts and attention.

Also true, though, is the fact that any activity or effort toward which we offer repetition grows in quality and becomes more consistent over time. If we give daily, uninterrupted time to the practice of gratitude, the reality of what we see, even amid challenges in our lives, becomes clearer. Without this practice we become bitter and live with negative attitudes that make a consistently courageous mindset impossible, no matter how desperately we desire it.

Consider this example:

If you want to turn on the lights and are sitting right now, you just need to get up and flip the wall switch to *ON*, right? While desiring optimism and positivity (lights on) is a choice, however, that choice won't matter if there is no electricity feeding the switch. We wire our switch and ensure electrical flow by getting the gratitude work done (paying the electric bill). This helps ensure that the output of our desire to choose optimism (flipping the switch) yields the result (lights on) that we expect, when we expect it.

As Paul wrapped up the fourth chapter of his letter to the Philippians, he ended with a statement of great conviction and belief, declaring that "I can do *all* [things] through him who gives me strength" (emphasis added). Inherent in this statement is a belief that there are no impossibilities in the presence of a God who is for you. It is in this strength of belief that all meaningful achievement begins. When we possess a conviction that comes from positive thoughts and attitude and proper perspective, there are few limits on what we can achieve.

What does it look like to train our minds to consistently operate with a conqueror's mentality? First, if you aren't failing at something, try harder. Just as comfort cannot yield growth, playing in the safe spaces where your wins are certain will not move you closer to realizing the best version of yourself. I have learned that it's important to step out of your comfort zone and take on real challenges. To do this we need to change the way we view failure.

Admittedly, this is hard to do when we buy the enemy's lie that God has left us "without" or that our failures will make us appear foolish in the eyes of others. This is why meditating on the provision and greatness of the Gift-Giver is so important. Focusing our thoughts on God's presence reminds us of His goodness, which provides us an assurance that we, as children of God, will never walk or fight alone in this life.

As previously stated, our perspective changes when we focus on God. We just need to get close enough to His glory. Once our attention is centered properly and a spirit of gratitude has molded our attitude, we will begin to see our perspective shift. The contentment that right attention and attitude yields changes not only how we perceive the size of our challenges but also our ability to overcome them. We'll now begin examining the two competing perspectives of abundance and scarcity. Only one of these perspectives will get us to a conqueror's mentality.

Let's begin with scarcity. A mentality of scarcity is rooted in the idea that our opportunities and the things we wish to acquire exist in fixed amounts and are usually in short supply. This belief limits possibilities, stifles progress, and creates a pursuit whereby the caving in to insecurities invariably wins and meaningful growth loses. When viewing life and its challenges through a lens of scarcity, I can be more concerned with hoarding the resources I possess and how comparatively good I look than with investing whatever is necessary to realize who I was created to be and what I was created to do. This is because truly getting good at something requires learning through trial and error, through making mistakes and wrong turns, which often humble us and can, we fear, leave us looking our worst.

In reality, the opposite is true. When I conquer the false notion of scarcity I can more effectively embrace uncertainty and challenge, overcome my fear of failure, and humbly learn from whatever short-term embarrassments might occur in the process of growth. If we point back to what we learned in the Identity chapter, however, we can see how living with a shaky identity foundation, rooted in craving the applause and approval of others, can yield a scarcity perspective, where insecurities (and the fear that results from them) rob us of peace and triumph.

The lens of abundance offers an entirely different perspective. In abundance, gratitude, creativity, and collaboration can thrive. A person living in abundance understands that they are not the sole generator of opportunity, nor is the totality of opportunity fixed or limited. Therefore, those living from a perspective of abundance often live with a humble, confident, and sober assessment of their skills, and these attributes have the largest influence on what they can become. Those who live out of an abundance mentality are also comfortable with who they are (and who they are not) and possess a firm internal conviction of their inherent worth and value. Most importantly, in abundance we see unlimited opportunity and possibility.

One passage of Scripture that emphasizes the abundance of life that is found in relationship with God was written by King David and is found in Psalm 23:

> The LORD is my shepherd, I lack nothing.
> He makes me lie down in green pastures,
> he leads me beside quiet waters,
> he refreshes my soul.
> He guides me along the right paths

for his name's sake.
Even though I walk
through the darkest valley,
I will fear no evil,
For you are with me . . .

You prepare a table before me
in the presence of my enemies.
You anoint my head with oil;
my cup overflows.
Surely your goodness and love will follow me
all the days of my life,
and I will dwell in the house of the LORD
forever.

Did you count the ways in which David expresses an attitude of gratitude by focusing his attention on truth? Right off the bat, he declares, "I lack nothing." David was a courageous king who reigned at the height of Israel's history, and from this "journal entry" we see how his abundance perspective fueled his growth mindset. This confidence also reveals the depth of relationship David had with God. He had experienced God's protection and provision, both in battles with lions and bears and in the refreshing and peaceful settings of green pastures and quiet waters. While an imperfect human like the rest of us, David nonetheless chose to walk with God and pursue His righteousness and Way.

David states, "I will fear no evil, for you are with me." He clearly believed that no matter what valley he might have to travel or what weapon his enemies might form against him, God's presence would not leave him. We, too, need this perspective when our enemy attacks. We simply cannot let his voice flourish and gain volume in our mental soundtracks. Instead, we need to familiarize ourselves with Scripture and live in constant awareness of the presence of God so that we can keep ourselves centered in His truth and live boldly, free of the disabling distraction that fear creates.

By reminding ourselves of who and whose we are, we can disarm fear and pursue our challenges with clarity and confidence. Declaring that "I will fear no evil," David was making a *choice*. He didn't suggest that the enemies and adverse circumstances he faced didn't present real opportunities for fear. He just announced that, despite those circumstances, he would choose not to be afraid. How was that possible? By recalling and shifting his focus to gratitude and praise in the presence of the almighty God who had promised never to leave him. We have the same choice to make. We can either fear failure or take courage and fight, knowing that God is with us. I think the choice is clear.

A WARRIOR'S PERSPECTIVE

Instead of seeing failure as catastrophic and leading to criticism and shame, we need to look at it for what it truly is. Failure is something every human encounters (perfection in this life is an illusion), and it can be construed as an event that gives us the opportunity to apply lessons learned to propel our forward progress in life. Before we continue, let's consider the definitions for *mindset* and *courage*, which will be our focus for the remainder of this chapter.

> **Mindset:** (a) A mental attitude or inclination. (b) A fixed or growth state of mind.

Courage: Mental or moral strength to venture, withstand danger, and confront fear.

Based on what we first assessed in this chapter, I would say that, just as our thoughts direct our attention and our attention dictates our attitude, so does our attitude influence our mindset (the fixed or growth state of mind that dictates our level of openness for the challenges we face). Furthermore, I believe that it's the quality of our mindset that determines whether we will live courageously (choosing above fear in the face of criticism and danger). To that point, let's look at a famous poem written by Teddy Roosevelt, titled "Man in the Arena":

> It is not the critic who counts; not the
> man who points out how the strong man
> stumbles, or where the doer of deeds
> could have done them better. The credit
> belongs to the man who is actually in the
> arena, whose face is marred by dust and
> sweat and blood; who strives valiantly;
> who errs, who comes up short again and
> again, who spends himself in a worthy
> cause; who at the best knows in the end
> the triumph of high achievement, and
> who at the worst, if he fails, at least fails
> while daring greatly, so that his place shall
> never be with those cold and timid souls
> who neither know victory nor defeat.

If it is a growth mindset we are seeking, a mindset that is required for anyone committed to living in courageous pursuit of the best version of themselves, we must be willing to step into unpredictable arenas of challenge. As we do so, we should expect both fair and unfair criticism. In her book *Daring Greatly,* Brené Brown observes, "When our self-worth isn't on the line, we are far more willing to be courageous and risk sharing our raw talents and gifts."

I couldn't agree with her more, and this is why knowing that our self-worth and value have been eternally defined for us by the Almighty, our audience of One, is so important. A courageous mindset that does not cower in the fear of failure or criticism can exist only where a rock-solid sense of identity is present. This is what allows us to bring a warrior's mindset into our arenas of challenge.

Throughout the Old Testament we find numerous stories of godly courage in battle. In perhaps the most famous example, we learn of David (the same David who authored Psalm 23) and his showdown with a formidable giant. Despite his youth and inexperience, David possessed an unwavering belief that he would, with God's strength, defeat the giant. When we look more closely at this encounter, we draw more insight into what a conqueror's mentality looks like.

First, David didn't pay any attention to lies coming from naysayers as he approached the battle scene. Second, his ability to speak confidently to his belief that he *would* (not *could*) defeat the giant created confidence in those around him, kings and soldiers alike. This serves as a helpful reminder that our words, whether only to ourselves or directed toward others, matter. Third, David was so confident in his spiritual armor and the physical skills he had developed through his day job as a shepherd and defender that he disregarded the conventional advice of those "experts" who were unfamiliar with his history.

Did hearing the roar of an enemy army create any doubt in David? Maybe, but, if so, his misgivings didn't last long. That is because he knew how to take his thoughts captive and make them obedient to truth, not to his feelings! Fourth and finally, we see that David was not intimidated by his more experienced and seemingly more powerful opponent. Why not? This was likely because he didn't see himself as the underdog.

For one thing, he believed he wasn't fighting alone. He *knew* the size of His God and believed that God's presence was both with and for him! Unquestionably, David believed in his heart what the Gospel writer Mark would voice so many years later:

> *"All things are possible with God."*
> MARK 10:27

It's also possible that his optimistic attitude created a mindset that helped make the giant's weaknesses clearer to him. After all, the giant was older and larger, and David did not intend to fight him in a style the burly brute was accustomed to. Malcolm Gladwell, in his book *David and Goliath: Underdogs, Misfits, and the Art of Battling Giants*, highlights the fact that Goliath likely had a form of gigantism that would have had a significantly negative impact on his sight, strength, and mobility as he aged.

David's bold confidence was evident in that he minced no words when speaking to the more experienced giant warrior before battle. We don't get the sense that he was stuttering or shivering in his sandals. He was bold and ready to put his best on the line for a greater purpose and trusted the rest to God. Once the time for talking was over, David came running toward Goliath, powered by courage and backed by God.

Once in the arena, David went on the offensive and reached for his stone just as he had done countless times before. Unfazed by the audience of Israelite soldiers shaking in their armor, David lifted his arm and slung the stone. It met its mark and struck the giant between the eyes, dropping him in defeat and creating the stage for David to bring glory to God and move closer to his God-given purpose.

We see similar stories of courage throughout Scripture. From Joshua to Gideon to Samson to Elijah, we learn of leaders and warriors who, while all flawed in some way, put their faith in a God who had promised them victory. Other passages remind us that, when we feel fear (the debilitating response to danger), those feelings are not from God. Instead, God wants to instill boldness, power, love, and the benefits of a sound mind (resulting from our regular habits) into the mentality of those who keep their focus on Him.

TRIUMPH OF ACHIEVEMENT

God wants each of us to lean *on* our identity in Him and *into* the mentality that results from our having victoriously proven the effectiveness of His Way in the battles with which we are presented. When we stack these victories and experiences, God receives glory and our confidence grows. The focus we then bring into our daily lives shifts from being rooted in scarcity and based solely on our daily survival to one that continuously praises God for His presence and the abundance with which He blesses us, while we direct our attention to thriving in this life, in pursuit of Him and of His purpose for us.

While we encountered our share of challenges during my three years as Athletic Director at Ann Arbor Skyline High School, our community did experience many successes as a byproduct of our shared commitment to focusing on what mattered most. These successes were seen in both the wholistic development of our student athletes and in competitive triumphs. During that time our young athletic department won several district, regional, and state championships across all Varsity sports, including City championships for football and basketball, and a national championship in Crew (eight-person team rowing for men and women). This variety is what high school athletics should be about, and we achieved that together.

I was so glad I had courageously pursued this opportunity even after the lesser version of myself had told me I had no business doing so. I give God all the glory for this outcome and hope my experience may encourage others to recognize that, when the enemy wants to remind us of past failures and shortcomings to prey upon our fears, good things can happen when we turn our eyes and attention upward. Fear doesn't stand a chance where God, and His perfect love and peace, are present. His truth trumps the enemy's lies, renews our confidence, increases our boldness, and allows us to move forward as the men God designed, for the sake of others.

In January of 2017 I was asked out to coffee by the father of a student athlete. His name was Dan, and he was the CEO of a holding company. Over a cup of coffee, he invited me to join his company to do a similar kind of work with his teams, leaders, and culture (his involvement was in Senior living, not education) to what he had witnessed me doing as the athletic director at Skyline. After the initial feeling of shock, I remember feeling honored and humbled by the fact that someone outside our department was seeing the value in what we did.

I also remembered feeling unsure this would be a possibility worth entertaining. I had never worked outside the realm of public education and would have to say goodbye to a retirement pension I had worked into for fifteen years—not to mention that I couldn't conceive what my life would be like without sports! I asked Dan for some time to talk with Samantha, think, and pray about it.

I was at a crossroads and wanted to make the right decision. While the nature of *this* crossroads in my career was far different from my earlier experience, the way forward, again, wasn't immediately clear. Despite the uncertainty, however, I knew that the past five years had molded me into a new person.

With my identity now centered on being a child of God and now possessing a forward-moving, courageous mentality, I was far more open to considering this than I ever would have been before. Now my most pressing question, considering my deeper understanding of who and whose I was and a renewed confidence, was *Am I living out my purpose?* Or more to the point, *What is my purpose?* These were questions I would prayerfully consider in the weeks ahead.

Railroad Metaphor: Preparing Your Tracks

Our Mentality in life is akin to the rails on a railroad track that will ultimately elevate us for forward movement in life. Just as the rails of a track guide a train engine quickly and efficiently along its path, so too will our mentality, influenced by the object of our focus and the quality of our thoughts, guide our actions. Our lives, after all, are always moving in the direction of our strongest thoughts.

Once the bedrock and stability (the ballast and sleepers—our Identity) are established, the presence of strong rails (our Mentality) serves as the tracks that enable us to move forward in our lives. Without strong rails, composed of right thinking, a positive attitude, and courageous mindset to guide our life's path, we are prone to getting stuck in our fears or derailed by distractions.

MENTALITY TAKEAWAY . . .

God's Presence and Perspective Give You Courage for Your Stand and Struggle!

The quality of your thoughts determines the quality of your life and the direction in which it will move. While God chose you, the thoughts that inform your attitude and mindset are yours to choose. If you choose to live apart from God and focus your thoughts on negative lies and temporary circumstances, you will develop a disposition of scarcity and fear. If you elect to live in God's presence and focus your thoughts on truth, however, you will develop a perspective of possibility, abundance, and courage that emboldens you.

QUESTIONS: Do you tend to think negatively or positively? If you're a believer, do you believe that anything is possible with God, even amid your challenges?

APPLICATION: Practice gratitude. While there are many ways to do this (journaling, expressing appreciation to others, praising God, etc.), we should include on the list expressing our thankfulness to God in quiet solitude. By removing distractions and focusing on the good, we defend our minds against lies. It is only during meditation and prayer that we can perceive our obstacles in proper proportion to God's greatness.

CHAPTER 3

THE CONQUEROR'S PURPOSE
Driving Out Darkness

*"Darkness cannot Drive Out Darkness; Only Light can do that.
Hate cannot drive out hate; Only Love can do that."*
DR. MARTIN LUTHER KING, JR.

As I considered Dan's offer for me to change careers at the age of thirty-seven, I couldn't help but reflect on the previous five years. While uncomfortable in so many ways, these years had been transformational relative to my growth as a person. I now began to dedicate effort and energy toward understanding the *Why am I here?* question as I considered this potential transition.

While the last career step I took had required me to overcome some self-limiting barriers (the fears of failure and of looking foolish to others), taking a step toward this opportunity would come with a cost. Given the fifteen years I had devoted to a career in public education (with corresponding retirement pension investment), and considering what we were building at Skyline, this decision wasn't going to be easy.

As I contemplated a transition, the question of *What's my purpose?* continually rose to the forefront. I remember calling my dad and him reminding me to "be cautious, because there is a lot of unknown, and you're halfway to your pension." He obviously wasn't wrong. As I prayed, though, I felt God asking me, "Do you exist for a pension . . . or a purpose?"

Most of us don't want to be without the resources we need to support our families and spend on some things we enjoy. For me, while the top-end prospects for earning in this new opportunity were significantly higher, there was still risk. During that time I leaned into Jeremiah 29:11–13, which says:

> "I know the plans I have for you," declares the Lord, "plans to prosper you and not to harm you, plans to give you hope and future. Then you will call on me and come and pray to me, and I will listen to you. You will seek me and find me when you seek me with all your heart."

This verse gave me assurance that God has both a plan and a *promise* for my life, and the same is true for you. This amazes me. Not only does the God of the universe sustain our physical lives with breath and heartbeat, but He does so with a unique purpose in mind for *every human soul* on this planet. This is why His blessing of *Purpose* is the best gift we can ever know.

Furthermore, He says that we can realize His promise of prosperity, hope, and a future in this life only if we, with our whole hearts, prioritize our pursuit of Him and His kingdom purpose for us. As a result of coming to this understanding, I wanted to go all in, to focus and seek Him as *the* goal, with faith that everything else would be added from there.

Have you ever wondered if what you were currently doing, whether it be through your employment or your life's work, was what you were supposed to be doing? Are you fulfilling your purpose, impacting others, and shining your light the way God intended you to? Or are you just going through the motions without joy or direction? It is when, and only when, you live your life in pursuit of knowing God and His purpose for you that the light you were given to shine glows its brightest for others and brings you His joy unspeakable in return. In his poem titled "A Splendid Torch," the Irish playwright and critic George Bernard Shaw shared similar thoughts:

This is the true joy in life,
the being used for a Purpose
recognized by yourself as a mighty one;
Then being thoroughly worn out
before you are thrown out on the scrap heap;
the being a force of nature
instead of a feverish little clod of ailments and grievances
complaining that the world
will not devote itself to making you happy.
I am of the opinion that
my life belongs to the whole community,
and as long as I live
It is my privilege to do for it whatever I can.
I want to be thoroughly used up when I die,
for the harder I work, the more I live.
I rejoice in life for its own sake.
Life is no "brief candle" to me.
It is a sort of *splendid torch* which I get to
hold but for a moment,
and I want to make it burn as brightly as possible
before handing it on to future generations.

Shaw's poem reminds me of a passage of Scripture that contains the greatest sermon ever preached. In Matthew 5:14–16 we read an excerpt from Jesus's famous Sermon on the Mount:

> "You are the light of the world. A town built on a hill cannot be hidden. Neither do people light a lamp and put it under a bowl. Instead, they put it on its stand, and it gives light to everyone in the house. In the same way, let your light shine before others, that they may see your good deeds and glorify your Father in heaven."

As we discussed in the chapter on Identity, we know that God's plan of salvation for each of us is based solely on His goodness, which means that our pursuits of Purpose and fulfillment don't bring value there. They *do* bring value, however, when they reveal our Creator's glory so that *others* can know a life that promises true prosperity, hope, and a future. As legendary college basketball coach John Wooden once said, "Joy begins where selfishness ends". This is exactly what Jesus modeled on earth, and it cannot be lost on the believer that our ultimate purpose and destiny on this planet are to become like Christ in that way: a full embodiment of God's light, not for our glory, but to be seen by others and offer hope in a hurting world.

Like the effects that are seen in the direct line of a solar eclipse, it takes only a bit of light to drive out the darkness when it seems to be dominating all we see. During an eclipse event you can look up toward the sun while the moon covers it fully and see that a mid-day darkness is cast. Looking directly at the eclipse (even without sunglasses) is possible, as only a faint ring of light may be seen as an outline to the moon. Then, as the earth's position rotates and as just a sliver of the sun's light is revealed, light returns to the atmosphere and the darkness created by the moon's covering is completely driven out, even before the eclipse itself is complete.

As Jesus taught, we've each been given a light to penetrate the darkness around us. For that light to shine it's brightest, however, we must aim to meet needs beyond our own. If you are in a season of transition, I'd encourage you to take an inventory of God's mission and calling for your life, in addition to the undeniable gifts and passions He has blessed you with. Once you begin to examine each of these variables, and how they align with one another in your life, God's dream for you will begin to come into focus. Additionally, as your vision begins to take shape, it's important to remember that pursuing our purpose is not equal to pursuing our comfort. In fact, the two are completely unrelated and many times it is our fleshly desire for growth-limiting comforts and amusements that stands between us and pursuing our purpose dreams.

Ultimately, our decision is about pursuing either the Way of God (Matthew 7:13–14), which calls us higher, toward sacrifice and sharing His love and light for others or the easy way of the world and darkness (Psalm 1), which leads us into a self-seeking, lonely, dissatisfying, frustrating, and painful, descent. Choosing the way of the world also means to neglect the greater mission, calling, gifts, and passions with which the Creator of the universe, whose handiwork pours forth speech of His power and greatness (Psalm 19), has prepared for you.

As C. S. Lewis suggests in his book *Mere Christianity*, making this negative choice is to forfeit the knowledge that true joy in life, as joy (not momentary happiness), cannot be found apart from the One who created it. To choose the Way of God, on the other hand, means to travel a path of impact for others in pursuit of godliness and of His predestined purpose on our lives.

To be clear, to become godly is not to become God. This is the enemy's oldest lie (Genesis 3:4–5), and he introduces it to us when our human ego is unchecked and we are filled with vanity and pride. To be godly simply means to embody His character, values, and attitudes, as outlined in the Identity and Mentality chapters of this book.

HIS MISSION AND CALLING

Webster's dictionary defines *mission* as a duty assigned to a person or group. For me, as a believer in Jesus's teaching that He is the Way, the Truth, and the Life, this means that my ultimate mission in this life is to get to know my God, grow to resemble Him, and make His Good News (gospel) known to others. The apostle Paul clarified this charge in Acts 20:24, where he summarized his mission as a Christ-follower:

My only aim is to finish the race and complete the task the Lord Jesus has given me—the task of testifying to the good news of God's grace.

In support of this mission and calling, St. Francis of Assisi, founder of the Franciscan order of the Catholic Church in the thirteenth century, famously said that all Christians can go about doing this by "preaching the gospel at all times—when necessary, using words". This statement reminds us that, while preaching and teaching have their places in fulfilling the Christian mission, they aren't the only ways to *live* the gospel message. In fact, many times our actions do far more to advance or defy the gospel message than our words ever will.

I, personally, had always found great meaning in being a teacher of young people. This was a career that I felt was worthwhile and that impacted others positively. When examining the company culture at Common Sail, I learned of their mission to deliver "the absolute best experience for every person in every interaction, every minute of every day." This was a mission I could get behind. Furthermore, being given an opportunity to influence the scalable delivery of this mission through leaders in a growing company, without the barrier of institutional red tape, was intriguing to me.

Are you contributing to a God-honoring mission today? Does that mission present you with opportunities to maximize your impact and benefit others? Does it align with your calling (with that strong inner impulse, driven by a conviction or divine influence)?

I had always felt an impulse to lead, and that inclination had been validated by external feedback time and again. As a kid I had rallied together other boys for the neighborhood football and baseball games. As a teen I had been chosen by peers for leadership roles, such as class president and team captain. In college I had led the charge to bring Athletes in Action to Michigan State Athletics, and I had always envisioned leading a family of my own. Now in my career I enjoyed using influence I had earned to bring others together in pursuit of a common goal. I knew that I'd always want to do this in one way or another, yet I felt as if I weren't doing it to my maximum potential in the athletic director role.

Over time a vision began to materialize of bringing leaders across cultures, backgrounds, and perspectives into an empowering understanding of their God-given identity, value, and worth and equipping them with teaching, tactics, and tools to apply the mentality necessary to maximize their impact. With the Common Sail offer I was being asked to spearhead the development of a leadership curriculum that would equip leaders to lead more effectively. It was clear that this opportunity and my calling were in alignment.

Understanding a calling looks different for everyone. For some the resonance is absolute and certain. For others the picture may be less clear and require deeper reflection. Either way, in considering your calling I encourage you to be honest about a vision and dream that is true to you (not one that necessarily wins you more praise and approval from others). While pursuing your calling will stretch you and create discomfort, it will also cause you to grow. For clarity, I would suggest praying and considering whether your vision is influenced by your audience of One, validated by those who know you best, and in alignment with your unique gifts as an individual—which we'll get to next.

MY GIFTS AND PASSIONS

I've heard it said that coaches exist to inspire and equip others to reach their fullest potential. I've seen both good and bad models of coaching. I remember at a young age signing up to coach YMCA teams and enjoying it. In high school I took the coaching of our girls' powder-puff team seriously. Even when I was playing football at MSU, I knew that I wanted to coach football and felt that pursuing this at the high school level made sense, given my desire to lead and raise a family. When I eventually had that chance to coach high school football I was beyond excited, and the ten years during which I was able to both lead and mentor those young men were incredibly rewarding.

When I became an athletic director (while I enjoyed leading coaches), those opportunities to directly impact young people were reduced. Furthermore, when I considered the athletic director's role for what it was, I began to wonder how I had become one. What I mean is that the job is very administrative (order the equipment/uniforms, coordinate the buses, schedule the opponents, etc.), which is not in line with my gifts. Fortunately, I was blessed with secretaries who did have strength in these areas, which paved the way for an efficient operation.

Where I excelled in the role (especially at Skyline) was in gathering community and coaches for events and initiatives to grow programs. I enjoyed our booster club and raising funds for our programs and created unique game and travel experiences for our coaches and student athletes. When I'd talk to other athletic directors about things we did, many asked why. This was a fair question, given that those functions were not a part of the job expectations for the role.

The more honest I became about the gifts and abilities God had given me, the less intimidating the prospect of stepping away from public administration became for me. After all, God's purpose had to be tied to the gifts and talents he had built into me, especially those in which (through education and experience) I had developed strength.

Will Mancini defines strengths well in his book *Younique: Designing the Life that God Dreamed for You* when he describes them as "your developed talents—skills that bring thrills to bosses, team members, and customers." For me these functions included speaking, creating, coaching, and inspiring others.

Are you using your talents today? Are you enhancing your natural gifts through education or experience? For every one of us, there are the things we do better than most, and when we work hard to refine those gifts we shine our light, bring glory to God, and do our part to reveal His kingdom on earth.

The final variable is *passion*. When our work is aligned with our natural interests and passions, time invested and energy offered don't deplete us. For me this was always tied to building teams and helping others see and reach their potential. This is why Dan's offer, while unconventional, was not illogical. As an engaged parent in my athletic department, he had seen something in me that I did not (for which I'll forever be grateful) and wanted me to help fuel his dream for Common Sail. Eventually, it became apparent that there was just too much alignment and opportunity in this offer for me to pass it up, so I accepted.

I remember feeling both excited and anxious during that time. I was excited to be wholeheartedly pursuing my God-given purpose by aligning my personal mission, calling, gifts, and passion in my day job and life's work, but also anxious about shoving off from a safe career shoreline that provided union privileges and perceived security.

Does the revelation of these four Purpose variables and of finding their alignment in pursuit of your individual purpose destination resonate with you? Have you taken time to consider any or all of these variables as they relate to performing your life's work? If not, there's no better time to start than now. You can begin by visualizing what it would take to begin moving toward that reoccurring vision or dream that exists in your soul. Then you can recall, or seek, the honest feedback of others relative to your unique gifts and determine how each of these variables intersects with your passions.

There is nothing better than living life on purpose and with intention, and using this approach to establishing yours can bring you the assurance that the direction in which you are moving is from your Maker and not the result of your chasing fleeting desires to earn the applause of others or to satisfy your fleshly wants.

FULFILLMENT IN PURPOSE

While Jesus Christ, with whom it is my goal and purpose to pursue relationship, was the perfect embodiment for me of living in pursuit of God-given Purpose, the desire to pursue fulfillment has been placed in the hearts of every human since the very beginning, meaning that these concepts are not exclusive to Christian thought. The writings of the ancient Greek philosophers Plato and Aristotle, who lived sometime in the fourth century BC, serve as evidence of this. They frequently discussed a concept they called *arete*, which could be summed up to mean "living up to one's potential," and suggested that this pursuit could offer people wholistic fulfillment. While they never outlined how this potential could be achieved or trained for, I believe the Bible helps us find this answer if this is truly what we're seeking.

Are you living up to your potential today? Have you experienced the difference between the momentary happiness that material pleasures and possessions can bring and the lasting joy that spending yourself in your God-designed purpose can afford? Or does the risk associated with pursuing your purpose hold you back? If so, that's only natural so you don't have to beat yourself up over it. If you need a nudge, however, I've always found one offered through a quote of one of my favorite authors, Mark Batterson, in which he says, "Quit living as if the purpose of life is to arrive safely at death!".

Perhaps you're thinking about how much your financial situation and status could change if you begin pursuing your purpose and changing your priorities accordingly. That prospect can be intimidating and feel risky, or even crazy. I get it. My advice is that you take the time to breathe and listen for God's still, small voice.

Remember, He has plans to prosper you and not to harm you. He doesn't want to bankrupt you or rob you of your earthly wealth and assets. He just wants to change your relationship to, and dependance on, those things so that He can take top priority in your life. If you're not intentional about determining your purpose and His dream for your life, you'll lack direction and forces outside your control will drive you toward their interests, robbing you of the joy of realizing your destiny and depriving the world around you of a light only you can shine.

As you consider all these challenges and questions, I recommend that you do one thing before all else: pursue Jesus Christ with your whole heart, mind, and strength. At the end of the day, this is what He wants most and when we do, things have a way of falling into place and for our good.

Railroad Metaphor: Deciding Your Direction

In the journey of our lives, there is a destination at which we were each designed to arrive and a dream that we were intended to realize. You need to discover and pursue yours or live with the regret of not doing so. In addition to training our hearts (Identity—foundation) and minds (Mentality— tracks) in truth, we must honestly assess and align our mission, gifts, calling, and passion if we want to live out God's Purpose for our lives. This is where we realize the impact that we were uniquely created to have on the world around us; it is therefore the purpose destination toward which we must point our tracks.

PURPOSE TAKEAWAY . . .

Jesus's Priorities and Promise Serve to Lead Your Search and Guide Your Steps.

Jesus, in His Sermon on the Mount, outlined simple priorities for those interested in discovering fulfillment through living out their God-given Purpose in this life. In Matthew 6 Jesus calls us to seek His kingdom and His righteousness, first. Our Lord summarized the entirety of God's law into two commandments, focusing not on the letter but on the spirit of the Old Testament law, which specify *how* we are to go about seeking His kingdom and righteousness: Love God and serve others (Mark 12:30–31). By our living out His priorities and aligning our mission, passions, gifts, and calling, God's promise and dream for our lives is revealed.

QUESTIONS: Have you identified your God-given gifts and passions? Do you see how they can provide insight into your calling and be used to help fulfill the Great Commission?

APPLICATION: Is there a vision or dream you revisit in your moments of reflection and times with God? If so, write it down. If not, begin to intentionally prioritize your life according to Jesus's outline and pray that His dream for you will be revealed. As this picture comes into focus, begin setting goals to serve as benchmarks for pursuing your God-given destiny.

CHAPTER 4

THE CONQUEROR'S LINKS

Sacrificing for Something Greater

"Life's most urgent question is . . . What are you doing for others?"
MARTIN LUTHER KING, JR.

Once I had determined to wholeheartedly prioritize the pursuit of Purpose in my life, my next steps were to find ways to apply my gifts and passions in the service of others and connect more meaningfully with a community of people and partners who could challenge and encourage me in that pursuit. We all need this if we are serious about reaching our purpose destination. For the believer this is where getting plugged in to a local church body of believers is critical. While it is true that church attendance has no bearing on our eternal salvation, it can have an immeasurable impact on our growth and success.

Furthermore, Scripture tells us that the church is God's way of displaying His glory and providing a platform within which believers can thrive as the carriers of His gospel to the world. Church should be a place where we personally practice the sacrificial love of God, not a place where we merely consume the fruits of everyone else's sacrifice.

LINKING UP

Let's examine the word *link*. A link is defined in the dictionary as "a relationship between two or more things, especially where one thing affects the other." The example offered is of a chain or a bond. Links exist to bring things together to fulfill a purpose, and so it is with our lives. We need reliable connections to help us fulfill our purpose of shining God's light through our gifts. Have you ever heard the phrase "You're only as strong as your weakest link"?

The truth is that life is a team game, and none of us will reach our purpose destination on our own. We can go so far as to invest the time to do the personal work that needs to be done to establish a rock-solid Identity, a courageous Mentality, and a Purpose-driven direction for our lives, but if we truly desire to realize our destiny the endeavor will also require engaging with the right team of people and partners in a healthy community.

In the right community the gifts and talents of members complement each other, and *fit* is found. Your best version can't be lived alone, and God designed it that way. It is certain that you will encounter times in your life when your vision is unclear and your understanding is limited, times when you will need wisdom from others to help you discern the right course of action. With so many self-serving belief systems in our world today, many of which suggest that truth is relative and that you should follow every feeling or inclination in your heart, it is critical for you to seek advice from those who will not only relate to your circumstances but also refer you back toward the truth of God, which points to sacrifice, family, and fellowship.

In addition to being supported by the Link traits of those with whom we associate most closely, living the link principle gives us opportunities both to serve others and to lead, which allows us the privilege of helping others win. This was modeled for us by Jesus throughout His ministry, as recorded in the Bible. His plan for impacting and changing the world with the Good News of the gospel was not achieved through scheduling a Sermon on the Mount concert tour. Instead, He chose to connect daily with twelve ordinary people, just like you and me, by meeting them where they were at. He then strengthened them through relationship and challenged them toward their shared mission through meaningful connection. In my humble opinion this is what makes Jesus's example of leadership the greatest of all time.

In fact, His leadership model served as the primary inspiration for the leadership curriculum I was hired to collaboratively build at Common Sail, to provide a framework and tools for leaders to effectively serve the people to whom they were responsible. These resources eventually reached leaders from each of the eight businesses that operated under our community umbrella (Experience, Wellness, Sales, Culinary, Enrichment, Maintenance, Housekeeping, and Administration) across our growing portfolio.

Looking back on my time at Common Sail, I recognize that this was the project I was most grateful to be a part of because I was applying meaningful lessons I had learned to assist others while honoring my calling to lead and use my gifts to educate, coach, and speak with a team of like-minded and talented individuals who together made it all go.

When we are a part of a team or group linked together by a common purpose, our gifts are elevated and enhanced by being complemented by the gifts and talents of others. In these groups learning increases, understanding grows, joy is experienced, and our causes are advanced.

This truth is reflected in nature, as well. There are many examples of species that travel in packs and benefit from group association. Wolves are one such species that thrive in packs. In the wild survival isn't assured, but the odds of it increase significantly when hunting, danger avoidance, and defense are practiced throughout the group.

The same is true in our lives. We as humans find ourselves "in the wild" more often than we may realize, and attempting to go it alone isolates us and leaves us susceptible to attack. We need a pack to run with! The poem I offer on this theme is one I first came across in college, and I was powerfully reminded of it at one of our Servant Leadership training events in Ames, Iowa.

Following is an excerpt from Rudyard Kipling's "The Law of the Jungle," which was shared by our Waukee, Iowa, Maintenance Director to emphasize the importance of a leadership team's ability to foster a "pack-like, have-each-other's-back" mentality in their site teams. The famous introductory excerpt to that poem reads:

> Now this is the law of the jungle,
> As old and as true as the sky;
>
> And the wolf that shall keep it may prosper,
> But the wolf that shall break it must die.
>
> As the creeper that girdles the tree trunk,
> The law runneth forward and back.
>
> For the strength of the pack is the wolf,
> And the strength of the wolf is the pack.

The remaining nineteen lines of this poem go on to tell the story of how the law, habits, and routines of the pack are essential for survival and must be obeyed. This poem has been used by countless sports coaches through the years who aim to place emphasis on the importance of loyalty and an unwavering commitment to the standards of the team and the teammates who share them. Why? Because they want their athletes to know that acting in alignment with the values of the team is always the best way to thrive, even when sacrifice is required.

Back in biblical times the apostle Paul knew the importance of building a strong team. After all, the only way the gospel message would thrive against unrelenting adversity was if new groups of believers were to forge a sense of "Be for Each Other" unity, togetherness, and common purpose. He also encouraged early church communities to work hard, care for each other, and allow for each other's faults. Simply stated, Paul knew that the best teams give and forgive! Without these "pack norms" churches would die, and the shared Good News to which many have given their lives would have been lost. Paul praises the fellowship of believers in Acts 2:42:

> "They devoted themselves to the apostles' teaching and
> to fellowship, to the breaking of bread and to prayer."

Through creating chemistry in these ways, we come to understand and respect each other better as different people, each created uniquely by God for a divine purpose. In his book *The Five Dysfunctions of a Team*, Patrick Lencioni says that the absence of trust comes from "an unwillingness to be vulnerable." I would agree. Trust doesn't happen just because a group of people are *asked* to trust each other. Trust is earned, and it requires honest communication and authentic connection; true leaders do whatever it takes to create the environment for this to happen, regardless of circumstances (as evidenced by the legendary San Antonio Spurs coach Greg Popovich in Daniel Coyle's book *The Culture Code*).

As we get to know those with whom we share community through "fellowship and the breaking of bread," we gain appreciation for one another's experiences, perspectives, and gifts and become willing to commit the best of ourselves for the sake of the cause. Over time, as we experience together the highs and lows and the sharing of forgiveness, challenges, failures, and successes, the bonds of solidarity are forged.

It is thus essential that we each find a community, team, group, or pack that shares a oneness of purpose to which we can contribute generously and from which we can benefit. This is our only hope to thrive in pursuit of our purpose. Are you engaged in a community or team today? If so, are you as a group aligned in your belief and mission? Does the living culture of the team reflect this alignment? Do you trust that everyone is committed to the goal? Are you?

WE ARE A BODY!

Once we are a part of a community that is aligned in belief, chemistry, and character, placing an emphasis on the development of a *we* over a *me* team spirit creates a strong standard that guides all interactions. Teams that put these puzzle pieces together through sacrificial love build a united sense of family and win. It's really that simple.

To illustrate this point, I'll reference the early Christian church in Corinth, Greece (near Athens, where athletes competed in the first Olympic games and where early Stoics debated philosophy). In the first of two letters he wrote to this group of new believers, Paul created a metaphor that compared the human body and its parts to the critical parts and traits of a team.

Why did he do this? He knew how important it was for this new body of Christians (along with other early church communities) to forge a loving sense of family and develop into a winning team if the greater mission of sharing the Good News of Jesus Christ throughout the pagan Roman Empire were to be realized and Jesus Christ's Great Commission fulfilled. If human nature were to have won out, church members would have placed their personal interests above the stated goals of the group, and the gospel message intended to reach the world would have died before it could ever have been shared on any meaningful scale. Paul's "body of Christ" metaphor is found in 1 Corinthians 12:12, 18–20, 27:

> Just as a body, though one, has many parts, but all its many parts form one body, so it is with Christ. . . . God has placed the parts in the body, every one of them, just as he wanted them to be. If they were all one part, where would the body be? As it is, there are many parts, but *one* body . . . Now you are the body of Christ, and each one of you is a part of it. (emphasis added)

In articulating his body metaphor, Paul underscored the fact that unity is not synonymous with uniformity by acknowledging that members of the body (people) are diverse and different but play equally important roles in carrying out the greater function of the body. Anyone who has ever attempted to bring a team together knows how important this point is. Think of any team you have been a part of. Can you recall arguments over who was the most important player or position or department? My guess is that most have. This is what happens when individual insecurities (especially in leaders) are prioritized above the team goal.

If a person doesn't possess a sense of worth from their audience of One (which makes possible an honest and humble assessment of their contributions and those of others), their human need for such recognition will have them looking for a sense of importance gleaned from others. As a result, they will undermine the mission, either consciously or unconsciously, as they gear their actions toward positioning themselves as more important than the whole.

When this happens the effects are like those of a musician in an orchestra deciding to showcase their instrument's individual notes in a setting where the harmony of all instruments and keys is the goal. The result is something that sounds like a sixth-grade symphony—hard for an audience to listen to and unable to deliver on the goal. Paul, the maestro of the early church, if you will, clearly needed to create harmony within the body of believers when he offered this metaphor, so that their collective sound would attract outsiders versus sending them away with their ears ringing in agony. So, what did he do?

Well, first, he reminded everyone that their specific gifts came from (God) and underscored the importance of their working collaboratively in the process of bringing those gifts to usefulness. As suggested in his letter to the Colossians, Paul believed that all members of the church body should work hard to effectively use their gifts, as though they were doing this for the Lord (which they were) and not men. Paul knew that, in teams and packs where there is idleness and me-first attitudes, selfish bickering that distracts from the goal is always present. In groups where there is an expectation to share our gifts in promotion of the goal through mutual hard work, on the other hand, there's less idle time and energy for unproductive behavior.

Second—the point at which we see his powerful metaphor unfold—Paul detailed the various gifts needed to move forward the mission of the church. In addition to identifying the need through his "body of Christ" metaphor, he emphasized the importance of each part and player while also highlighting how each part needed the other to achieve the collective purpose. His metaphor painted a simple and rational picture of his vision, while his message of inclusion and importance fed the hearts of those needing to feel a sense of true belonging and togetherness. An absolute masterclass in leadership!

SACRIFICIAL COMMITMENT

In the next and thirteenth chapter of his first letter to the church at Corinth, Paul speaks to the importance of what he described as an indispensable element of any thriving body: *love*. In this chapter the apostle describes a sacrificial love that never fails— or always wins. In his long list of descriptions of sacrificial love, one descriptor in particular highlights the "*we* over the *me*" element that is found in all thriving teams: "not self-seeking." Demonstrating this in any setting, professional or personal, is nearly impossible in our human nature. At times this means fewer accolades, less acknowledgment, or maybe even the sacrifice of our personal desires. The reality is that, if the "*we*" goal is most important, our "*me*" goals must take second place.

Allow me to add to Paul's "body of Christ" metaphor to bring this point home. As complex and miraculous as the bodies God gave us are, they are dead without blood pumping through them. When we join chapters 12 and 13, we see that it's the presence of God's sacrificial love (demonstrated through Christ's shed blood during His crucifixion) that serves as the lifeblood required for the church body to have life.

We can conclude from this that the defining characteristic of God's love (our lifeblood), is *sacrifice*. Scripture reminds us that there is no greater demonstration of love than to lay down one's life for a friend, and Jesus modeled this. While this truth may not always lead us to lay down our physical lives for one another, it will most certainly call us to lay down our personal desires and pride in favor of the greater good.

Cultures that live (not just talk) *selflessness* offer benefits that others simply do not. Qualities like generosity, forgiveness, healthy conflict, encouragement, truth, and grace abound where *sacrificial love* is the standard. Finally, if you aspire to reach your full potential and arrive at your God-given purpose destination in life, I encourage you to be an active member of a local church where this culture is experienced. Belonging to a body of believers (though human and therefore imperfect) is essential to experiencing a fullness of joy in our life here on earth.

WALKING WITH THE WISE

Just as engaging with the right community is important, we also must be selective with the individual partners with whom we choose to invest our time. To know whether we are engaged in the right partnerships, we must first ask ourselves whether the person we are when we are around such people is a better or lesser version of who we can be. Are we built up or torn down in their presence? Are we challenged or weakened? Are we inspired toward humility and faith or nudged toward vanity, arrogance, and pride?

Being honest with ourselves when we take this inventory is the first step toward determining whether our friendships will get us closer to our purpose or drive us further from it. Through the right partnership bonds of friendship, we can find compassion and understanding during times of challenge, suffering, and loneliness. Therefore, picking quality mentors and friends is important.

Simply stated, quality partnership moves us closer to our goals and makes us better versions of ourselves. Through God's providence, some friends will be placed in our lives for a reason, others for a season, and some for a lifetime. While there are certainly times when we need compassionate support in friendship, we should also acknowledge those times when we need inconvenient wisdom and healthy confrontation to sharpen us. One expression of this reality is found in Proverbs 27:17:

As iron sharpens iron, so one person sharpens another.

I first encountered that verse when I was playing football at Michigan State. My friend Josh and I had started a Bible study, and that particular Scripture had become a focal point we ended up sharing with our Strength and Conditioning coach, who decided to make it a slogan of the Spartan Football Culture, plastering "Iron Sharpens Iron" all over the weight room and football. For the next twenty years that phrase embodied the essence of the Spartan Brotherhood.

This biblical wisdom was in alignment with so many of the lessons that he and other coaches wanted to teach us. We could be great as a team only if the individual relationships within the group spurred us on, through challenge and encouragement, to demonstrate sacrificial love for one another and help each other become our best versions, both on the field and off.

I believe that it is very rare for a person to fall into "iron links" by chance. I also believe that the criteria for forging a strong link are not always easy to attain. For instance, I've spent time around talented and financially wealthy people who were still dominated by their insecurities; looked out only for themselves; and, therefore, weren't very strong links at all. On the other hand, I've also been around people from humble means who are genuine; don't possess material wealth, but function as the very definition of "salt of the earth" (Matthew 5:13); and can be relied upon in any situation.

Since the surface indicators don't always point us in the right direction, establishing criteria for those with whom we should spend significant time is important. Consider Jim Rohn's Average of Five Rule, which suggests that we become the average of the five people we are closest to. Have you seen evidence of this concept in your life or in the lives of others? When you consider your "circle of five," does it consist of strong, wise, honorable, and dependable links of function and integrity? If so, great. If the answer is no, or you're not sure, you likely have some partnership decisions to make, hopefully sooner rather than later.

We all encounter confusing crossroads that have the potential to significantly influence the trajectory of our lives. If you think back to times in your life when quality advice was offered and received, did acting in accordance with that advice keep you pointed in the right direction and improve your situation? How about bad advice? Have you taken, or acted upon, any of that? If so, I'm guessing that it set you back; otherwise, you wouldn't have determined in hindsight that the advice was bad.

I have found myself in both situations. When I think of times when I received good advice, it wasn't always what I wanted to hear in the moment, but it was offered by a trusted friend or mentor who knew me and shared experiences of their own that imparted valuable wisdom. This allowed me to make wise decisions based on solid principles versus shifting, fleeting emotions. When I have followed trails of bad advice, I have been lacking in wisdom, and instead of keeping me on track to achieve purpose goals the outcome either benefited the advice-giver most or encouraged me to chase and satisfy momentary desires.

For these reasons we will lean into Proverbs 2 to serve as the outline for our "Iron Criteria." At the start of this chapter of the Bible, we see that the author implores us to tune our ears to wisdom and ask for understanding. Therefore, we will identify *wisdom* as Iron Criterion #1. Before the author lists the practical benefits of wisdom, he reminds us that all wisdom comes from God and that we would benefit from pursuing Him first, since "from his mouth come knowledge *and* understanding" (emphasis added).

In a world where so much knowledge abounds, the wisdom needed to understand how to best apply that knowledge seems so rare. In many cases it is knowledge that can bring us worldly power and wealth, but those things alone cannot afford the joy we assume they will. Whereas those who have wisdom, regardless of their status, can see through a God-powered lens and view things for what they truly are.

Therefore, when we receive wisdom from God and plant ourselves in environments along with others who do the same, we improve our chances for meaningful growth. In adding these variables, along with a soil of godly character and love in our hearts, the seeds of confident mentality, a perspective of possibility in our minds, and the pursuit of God's light in our work, we give ourselves a chance to flourish.

In Proverbs 2 we also learn about steering clear of evil and immoral people, about following the steps of goodness and staying on paths of righteousness. While we may observe the evil and immoral profiting for a season, their demise is inevitable. Not only does walking with wise partners keep us on the good path and away from enemy traps, but it also propels us toward our purpose through the benefits of loyalty, listening, curiosity, advocacy, encouragement, and accountability. When we walk with the wise we become wiser ourselves. With that said, let's take a closer look at the remaining Iron Criteria.

First, *loyalty* (#2). If you are interested in being a person of conviction who pursues doing right, you *will* at times be unpopular, encounter hardship, and earn the criticism of others. During these seasons it is good to be supported by allies who see you as an individual apart from what you have, your gift, or what you do and won't leave you by yourself as soon as it becomes inconvenient to associate with you. People who are loyal remain faithful and committed, no matter how uncomfortable it may at times be to do so.

The friendship traits of *listening* and *curiosity* (#3 and #4) are also key. If someone doesn't listen or take the time to ask thoughtful questions, they're simply not interested in what matters to you and therefore won't be able to consider your perspective or empathize with your experience. It's only through listening and being curious that we can hope to relate.

In addition to listening and curiosity, *advocacy* (#5) is the next level and another valuable trait of a friend. In life there are times when our ability or word is not enough to move us forward in a pursuit. Friends who will go out of their way to act on our behalf, while creating opportunities for our growth, are the ones we want to stick closely to. They want to see us living in our best version, and their actions, beyond just their words, back this up.

Finally, the best friends provide the right balance of *encouragement* and *accountability* (#6 and #7). When times get tough an encouraging word from a friend can go a long way. An encouraging friend reminds you who, and whose, you are and delivers when some confidence-boosting feedback is needed to increase your confidence. On the other hand, they will also hold you accountable (iron sharpens iron style) when they know what your best looks like but see you acting beneath it.

If you're able to add individuals with these traits to your inner circle and distance yourself from the wrong company (those with questionable character), your connections will help strengthen your character and keep you pointed toward your God-given purpose destination. When we engage in these types of friendships, we also get the opportunity to *be* a friend and mentor in support of others. In many cases it is first through giving of ourselves and being a friend that we discover the benefits of having a friend.

As we build our network of trusted friends, we need to remember that we all have one Creator and have been given the amazing opportunity to enter relationship with Him through Jesus Christ. He is the Vine, and we are the branches hoping to bear fruit. Therefore, if you want to deliver the impact you were created for, you must remain in constant connection with Him, *linked* with Him first. Apart from Him we are nothing and can do nothing. He alone knows exactly what we need to live out the purpose He designed for us.

Railroad Metaphor: Connecting the Rails

Here's a quick review of what we've established so far: (1) Our rock-solid foundation (ballast) is our Identity. (2) To support steady forward movement in our lives, we need quality tracks (rails) that can consistently and reliably guide our focus and direction. This is our Mentality. (3) Our direction should point toward our goal (destination) and be dictated by the alignment of our gifts, mission, calling, and passion, which combine to form our Purpose. This brings us to the next stage of our metaphor, the fasteners.

On a railroad all prior components in our metaphor (ballast, sleepers, and rails) must be set and linked together to elevate us above shifting terrain and enable us to withstand external elements. This function is executed by the fasteners, which include a diverse combination of plates, clips, spikes, and joints. (4) In our metaphor these fasteners (Links) that hold our track together are comparable to the types of connections (friendships, partnerships, packs, teams, communities, etc.) we establish in our lives. Just as the fastening clips and spikes are essential to the connection and reliability of a railroad track and its function, so are the people and partnerships to whom we link ourselves on our journey. Our life's rails will be only as strong as the links we choose to support them with.

LINK TAKEAWAY . . .

God's People and Partners Can Serve as Your Support and Aid in Your Success.

Humans were designed by God to be relational and therefore need to be a part of a broader community of people to reach their full potential. No one ever wins on their own. It is impossible to do so. We need to be a part of a broader community connection, where we also find "iron sharpens iron" partnerships that provide opportunities for us to refine and share our gifts in the service of others. When we are part of a community like this, our links keep our tracks connected and pointed in the direction of our destiny, so that we can pursue the God who designed the plan for us to realize.

QUESTIONS: Are you actively involved in a community of believers today? If not, what's holding you back? What can you do to set aside your reservations and excuses and get connected?

APPLICATION: Take some time to consider whether spending time with those in your inner circle moves you closer to or further from your goals and the person God made you to be. Commit to assessing this regularly and, more importantly, making the social decisions necessary to ensure that your inner circle is of the "iron sharpens iron" variety.

CHAPTER 5

THE CONQUEROR'S ENDURANCE

Persevering through Trials

"Don't judge me by my successes,
but by how many times I fell and got up."
NELSON MANDELA

Hardships, setbacks, and difficulties should be expected on life's journey. While none of us desires to go through the valleys of adversity that darken our days, disrupt our comforts, and burden our souls, God uses our pain and trials as a part of His process to make us complete and capable of living out the purpose He has uniquely designed for us, *if* we endure. Enduring effectively, however, requires waiting patiently, with disciplined persistence and obedient perseverance. We must learn the virtues of patience and discipline and live in obedience to His commands in the face of the confusion, pressure, delays, and adversity that can shake our belief.

Furthermore, we should be aware that it is in these very seasons that our enemy wants most to tempt us, appealing to our weakness and human nature to temporarily ease our pain through means that would only bring on greater suffering, so that he can derail our pursuit. How we respond to these tests reveals the condition of our character at that given moment.

If we are unable to persevere obediently under the intensity of the refining heat, we delay the receipt of the blessings God wants to give us until we are provided another opportunity to pass our test. If we maintain our discipline, however, and allow His process to mold us, we become better equipped and prepared to carry a greater load along the Way to our purpose destinations, which introduces us to the fullest joy we can experience on this side of eternity.

WHY PAIN?

Why does a loving God allow pain? Why can't our experience on this earth just be filled with ease, comfort, and pleasure? It has been said that life *is* suffering. Whether the suffering is emotional, intellectual, financial, social, physical, spiritual, or some combination of these, life's trials and tribulations bring us pain, discomfort, and difficulty. I have come to believe that our storms and trials, and the sufferings we endure through them, are part of a divine process designed to strengthen and mold us. James 1:2–6 enjoins us,

> Consider it pure joy, my brothers, and sisters, whenever you face trials of many kinds, because you know that the testing of your faith produces perseverance. Let perseverance finish its work that you may be mature and complete, not lacking anything. If any of you lacks wisdom, you should ask God, who gives generously to all without finding fault, and it will be given to you. But when you ask, you must believe . . .

Three things stand out to me in this short yet powerful Scripture: (1) James (Jesus's brother) leads by saying that we should consider the trials and suffering we encounter in this life as *pure joy*. (2) His next clause, "whenever you face trials," make it clear that life's trials are a matter of *when*, not *if*. (3) We need wisdom from God. Not only can He identify with the experience of suffering (God the Father watched His Son being tortured, and Jesus Christ Himself endured the cross), but He is fully aware of all that is contributing to our confusion and wants to offer us understanding in our struggle, to help us grow *through* our trial with a hope that can anchor our soul.

The entire book of Job, which happens to be the first book in The Old Testament's series of poetic books of Wisdom, provides another reminder that no one (Job was the most morally upright and socially respected citizen of his day) gets through this life without facing trials. Job had to deal with unimaginable loss and endure extreme physical anguish—and yet, with a God who never left his side, he endured and persevered faithfully.

STRENGTHENED BY TRIALS

Whether it is through our personal experience or the stories of others, we have no shortage of reminders that trials, struggle, and the suffering that results from them are inevitable realities of our existence. While our enemy intends these troubles to destroy us, our loving and almighty Creator wants to use them for our good. While we may wish that there were a different Way to live on purpose and reach our potential, life teaches us that there simply isn't. Suffering is inevitable, and our ability to endure through it will determine whether we can realize what we were intended to

experience on the other side of it. The poem "Good Timber" by
Douglas Malloch offers perspective on suffering:

> The tree that never had to fight
> For sun and sky and air and light,
> But stood out in the open plain
> And always got its share of rain,
> Never became a forest king
> But lived and died a scrubby thing.
>
> The man who never had to toil
> To gain and farm his patch of soil,
> Who never had to win his share
> Of sun and sky and light and air,
> Never became a manly man
> But lived and died as he began.
>
> Good timber does not grow with ease,
> The stronger the wind, the stronger trees,
> The further sky, the greater length,
> The more the storm, the more the strength.
> By sun and cold, by rain and snow,
> In trees and men good timbers grow.
>
> Where thickest lies the forest growth
> We find the patriarchs of both.
> And they hold counsel with the stars
> Whose broken branches show the scars
> Of many winds and much of strife.
> This is the common law of life.

It's clear that Douglas Malloch learned the value of enduring through suffering, pain, and waiting. Life will continuously present you and me with opportunities to endure that can add to our toughness and grit (defined by Angela Duckworth as the "power of passion and perseverance for long-term goals"), not only for our own benefit but for the benefit of others who either rely on us or are inspired through our response to our challenges.

One such example that I witnessed came during the height of the COVID pandemic in 2020. During that time, I watched a difficult trial test, but not break, caregivers across our Senior living business. During the pandemic our caregivers and other front-line staff lived and served each day in conditions that none of us would wish for. They daily risked their personal health and well-being to serve our Senior residents, many of whom were dealing with the frustration of being disconnected from their loved ones.

While this display was inspiring, the toll COVID took on all our people was equally real. At the same time as our teams leaned into one another and found new ways to more effectively deliver excellent care, that struggle served to strengthen and improve our organization collectively, validating Malloch's assertion of what creates "good timber."

What storms of life have you endured or are enduring today? Our ability to understand that our trials are serving to mold us into more complete versions of ourselves can enhance our ability to overcome adversity. Maybe you haven't handled adversity as well as you'd hoped to. You might even have cursed God, turned to disobedience, or quit at some point. If that is the case, know that God still loves you and wants you to try again. He is still able to make you complete and fulfill His purpose for your life.

You just need to get up, repent, reset, and keep going! In these times it is helpful to remember God's promise that He will never allow our enemy to tempt us beyond what we can bear (1 Corinthians 10:13). No matter what we're facing we're never alone, and we *can* endure! Looking back on God's faithfulness also brings hope. Furthermore, when I *choose* to praise Him during these times I invite His presence into my struggle and demonstrate my faith that He will make a Way for my triumph.

In the big picture I see that the ups and downs of my journey are simply signs of life (think of an EKG here). Therefore, I can experience the joy of knowing that life's valleys are mere legs along my journey toward a mountaintop that has been prepared just for me. Given that certainty, using my energy to complain to God or others seems like an enemy-validating waste of time. Praising God instead, even when His ways are beyond me, helps me turn my outlook toward the promise of better days and the Giver who brings them.

WORTH THE WAIT

If we're strong enough to believe that bitter times will be followed by better ones, then we need to obediently persevere as we wait out, and grow through, the storms of our lives, knowing that the best is yet to come. We must come to believe that the best things "come to those who wait" and that our greatest wins exist on the other side of our waiting. Unfortunately, the uncertainty of waiting can be the hardest part, but what it equips us for makes the apparent delay worth it. In his letter to the Colossians, chapter 1:9–12, Paul reminds Christ's followers,

We continually ask God to fill you with the knowledge of his will through all wisdom and understanding that the Spirit gives, so that you may live a life worthy of the Lord and please him in every way: bearing fruit in every good work, growing in the knowledge of God, being strengthened . . . according to his glorious might so that you might have great *endurance and patience,* and giving joyful thanks to the Father, who has qualified you to share in the inheritance of his people in the kingdom of light. (emphasis added)

In a culture that feeds our desire for instant gratification, placing a value on the limbo of waiting can seem lazy or foolish. Nonetheless, the elimination of chaotic hurry and the willingness to lean into persistent godly disciplines sustain us during our seasons of inertia. Waiting also yields the harvest of patience and clarity for those who, when tested, reveal their heart's position toward their Creator, revealed in obedience. Not only do seasons of waiting prepare us for arrival at our purpose destinations by building patience, but they also build our faith.

Without faith we find ourselves unwilling to wait for God's best, and without patience we are unable to persevere during our waiting. The significance of patience and faith in the human experience was validated in a delayed-gratification study conducted by Stanford University researchers back in 1970. In this study, in a classroom of children each was individually offered a choice of either one marshmallow today or two tomorrow. A combination of the two options was selected by these students. The scenario gets interesting when we see the results of a follow-up study done during these same kids' adult years. What researchers discovered through this experiment was that the children who chose to patiently delay their gratification had consistently better life outcomes when considering the metrics of overall physical/ mental health and financial earnings. This study proved that waiting patiently and faithfully yields wins.

DISCIPLINED PERSISTENCE AND OBEDIENT PERSERVERANCE

Now that we have established that our biggest wins are on the other side of our faithful and patient waiting, let's dive into the *How should we wait?* question. While the first part of that answer is patiently and faithfully, the next parts, rooted in discipline and obedience, call for *action* during our waiting.

Before we discuss such action, however, I'd like to offer a thought. While God uses the waiting seasons in our lives to mold and mature us, we add undue stress and carry unnecessary weight when the enemy deceives us into believing that missing the mark in our discipline and obedience (a.k.a., *sin*) should drive us away from God in guilt and shame. The reality is that believing this lie can bring on additional and unhealthy emotional, mental, and physical distress.

When a flaw or shortcoming in our character is revealed, we need to carry our sin directly to God and seek His forgiveness in repentance, sooner rather than later, and then commit to new habits that will yield growth in that character area. When your discipline fails you and your human knowledge fools you, don't let these setbacks grow, snowball, and defeat you! As you get back to your feet, remember that your journeys and stories are unpredictable and abstract, more like a Picasso painting than a Rockwell. Nonetheless, when we hold to the Conqueror's

Way and walk daily with our Maker and Savior, our journey undeniably leads to the destination He has prepared for us, in His perfect timing.

For each of us, lessons in discipline are learned at various stages. In my journey I have learned that the gifts I've been given by God are elevated and sustained by discipline. Without discipline (and a clarity of vision that demands my persistence), gains made in the development of my gifts are lost to complacency, and I am easily discouraged when I am required to wait or endure hardship as I work toward my goals. Without discipline it's too easy to quit when the going gets tough, giving up what I want most for what I want in the immediate moment. Instead, I must remember that God allows *rain* in my experience only to grow me and that He still *reigns* during those storms. The hope that results is what I hold on to.

In addition to holding onto this hope, I have found that an initial neutral response to hard times and events can be helpful in the effort toward sustaining discipline. The best explanation of what I mean by *neutral response* can be found in Ecclesiastes 7:14, 18–19. In this passage King Solomon offers the following wisdom:

> When times are good, be happy;
> but when times are bad, consider this:
> God has made the one
> as well as the other. . . .
> It is good to grasp the one
> and not let go of the other.
> Whoever fears God will avoid all extremes.
>
> Wisdom makes one wise person more powerful
> than ten rulers in a city.

While much easier said than done, learning to adopt this neutral view when presented with undesirable circumstances and happenings helps keep me from spiraling into either frustration or panic, which often rob us of our chances to grow our faith through challenging times. The COVID pandemic taught me, as a business leader, firsthand the effectiveness of neutral response and disciplined persistence amid adversity. During COVID our business was presented with adversity that threatened our survival. Many of the difficulties we faced were brought to our doorstep by factors beyond our control, while in other cases systemic organizational flaws were revealed and magnified by the conditions COVID created.

It was during this season, in February of 2021, that Dan, our CEO (who was tested with incredible adversity) asked me to lead the operations side of our StoryPoint Senior Living business. Fortunately, the prior four years, spent serving leaders across those eight functions of our business mentioned in the last chapter, prepared me for this by creating inroads to vital relationships and insights into several challenges our business was facing.

Thanks to the hard work of so many caring, competent, and gritty people, we were collectively able to shift our energy away from obsessing over the doom and gloom scenarios that could have paralyzed us in excuse-making and defeat to instead accepting our situation for what it was and applying our efforts toward plugging the specific people and process holes that actually threatened to sink our ship.

By doing this we wasted less time on unproductive pursuits and expended our energy on the priorities that mattered most, which made a positive impact on our business and changed our trajectory while providing solid footing for future growth. While the specifics of our approach were neither riveting nor exciting, they reveal a great deal about the importance of neutrality and discipline in achieving successful outcomes in difficult times.

Considering obedient perseverance, we learn that Webster defines *obedient* as "subject to will of authority" and *perseverance* as "doing something despite failure, difficulty, or opposition." When we combine these terms, to exercise Obedient Perseverance is to subject ourselves to the will of an authority despite difficulties or opposition. While the strength we acquire through struggles makes patience and perseverance possible, persevering productively and enduring effectively happen only when we are obedient to the will and laws of God.

It is only in our obedience that we can see clearly, gaining the ability to discern God's will and direction in our pursuits. So, why is remaining obedient so hard? I believe the answers are pride and comparison. Our pride creates in us an arrogance that refuses to acknowledge our need to remain obedient to the Author of life itself. Comparison then distracts us when we take our attention off the race God intended for *us* to run and look to what other people *appear* to be experiencing in their races.

They *seem* happy, even though it doesn't look as if obedience is a part of their formula. So, we compromise for the quick reward, enslaving ourselves to our flesh, just to find out that the short-term happiness that pleased us doesn't convert to the lasting joy our souls long for. If we truly want to experience joy, we must see through the illusion of choice. Experiencing joy takes what it takes—obedience to Him.

In the Old Testament book of Daniel, we read about three men who demonstrated obedience to their God when they refused to bow to a foreign king and were thrown into a blazing furnace as a result. Despite the king's attempt to kill them, they obediently persevered (they were *joined by God* in that furnace) and survived. Once they were released from the furnace, the king publicly praised their God and promoted them to high positions in his empire. These men, held to the fire with their lives at stake, chose to be obedient, even if they would be put to death for that obedience. What can we learn from their story?

First and foremost, no matter how intense the heat of the fire you are in, know that you are not alone. God will always be with you. Second, don't compare your situation to that of others who may seem to benefit from taking the easy road. Instead, remain committed to God and to your obedience even through a fire that was intended to destroy you, knowing that your obedience will be used to bring glory back to Him. As we "run our races" we will suffer, and it can be tempting to compare our situations to those of others. We need to resist this temptation; otherwise, as Teddy Roosevelt warned, "Comparison will thieve our Joy."

Finally, as we abstain from compromise and comparison while we obediently persevere, we need to avoid giving in to the greatest temptation, which is to quit. Instead, we must hold on to the hope that we *will* obtain His promise for us and press forward. This is why dedicating the time and energy necessary to understanding, with clarity, His unique mission and calling for our lives is so important. If we are *certain* of the promise that we hold, we are far more likely to remain persistent in the disciplines of prayer, Scripture reading, gratitude, hard work, doing good, encouraging others, giving generously, patience, faithfulness, and praise, secure in the assurance that He who promised is faithful!

While we all *want* growth, we are not often eager to do what it takes to achieve those rewards. When it comes to discipline, our inconsistent attention, our discomfort, and our fleeting interests make follow-through and obedient perseverance hard. Nonetheless, if we can respond neutrally to adverse events and dedicate ourselves to spiritual disciplines, we give ourselves a better chance to keep the faith.

No matter what, we must be reminded that God hears our prayers and will provide, just as He has throughout our lives. This is why we can and should praise Him in *advance* of his deliverance and the passing of our test. Furthermore, Scripture tells us that when we feel trapped by our circumstances, it is praise that invites God into our struggle, breaking chains and bringing down walls. We must remain active in praise as we lean into our disciplines and overcome temptation, so that we can endure while we wait as He prepares us for His promise in His perfect timing. Unfortunately, aiming to do this on our own is a dead end. Not to worry, though; we'll address this in our next chapter.

Railroad Metaphor: Forming the Engine

To this point we have laid our forward-moving tracks (Mentality) on a rock-solid foundation (Identity) that points us in the direction of our destination (Purpose). Additionally, we have fastened together the rails of our track and secured them to our foundation by establishing reliable relationships and engaging in supportive community (Links). We now need an engine that is fit to ride these rails and endure the changing landscape and conditions along the Way.

Just as the assembly of a train engine requires an intense, white-hot heat to melt down the iron that is to be re-formed into a useful and productive shape, so do the painful trials in our lives serve to shape and mold us. Sometimes we feel forgotten and forsaken in this process, to the point that we are tempted to quit, but we can't. At the end of our tunnels of adversity and suffering exists a fullness of joy that is reserved for those who persevere.

The initial locomotive assembly process was well thought out and time consuming. The effective completion of that process required patient waiting, discipline, obedience, and faith. So, it is with our lives. God's process for shaping us is equally well thought out and requires His timing in order to be achieved.

While the heat of life's suffering and trials melts us into a substance that can be molded for a greater purpose, it is our discipline and obedience that serve as the frames into which our heat-softened "metal" is poured to take on permanent shape. We must patiently wait, enduring God's process for molding and strengthening us with discipline and obedience, if we are to receive the reward of His promise.

Without discipline and obedience, aided by neutral response, we are rendered formless when melted and poured out. If we want our purpose to be served through our suffering, we must remain faithfully obedient, not to our feelings or temptations but to God's commands. When we obey with discipline, the pounding and pressing that the boilermaker of life inflicts on us don't destroy us. Instead, they stamp and forge our character to take on His own shape, which alone can endure all the elements we are certain to face along the Way to our purpose destinations.

ENDURANCE TAKEAWAY . . .

God's Process and Preparation Build Strength and Stamina to Successfully Complete Our Journey.

We should expect adversity and suffering as guaranteed parts of life. The pain that results from our trials, however, is part of a divine process for molding us into Christ's likeness so that we can persevere through adversity and experience a fullness of joy made available only to those who can endure in the faith. In times of adversity, we must patiently endure, having faith that God's ways and timing are best, even as we wait. Your enemy wants to use these seasons of tribulation to derail your purpose pursuit, but God wants to prepare and equip you with stamina and strength for it!

QUESTIONS: Are you weary from a personal struggle that has left you carrying a burden you were never intended to carry? How has trying to remain obedient during this time tested you?

APPLICATION: Take an inventory of the spiritual disciplines you are tempted to neglect during hard times (including Scripture reading, prayer, praise, meditation, serving others, and connecting with other believers). Commit yourself to renewing, or doubling down on, these practices and chart the ways in which you have learned and grown, becoming more complete, during this time.

CHAPTER 6

THE CONQUEROR'S SURRENDER
Trust and Transformation

"Without the spirit of God, we can do nothing; we are as ships without wind, chariots without steeds, like coals without fire."
CHARLES SPURGEON

The Railroad Metaphor Recap:

1. Our Identity is established on a rock-solid foundation (ballast and sleepers) for our journey. *CHECK*
2. Our courageous Mentality provides a balanced and reliable rail base upon which we can move forward. *CHECK*
3. We have decided to move toward our Purpose destination, based on our unique mission, calling, gifts, and passion. *CHECK*
4. Quality Links (people and partners) keep our railway firmly fastened to our foundation and all its connecting parts. *CHECK*
5. The engine (us) that must travel this railroad network has Endured an intense molding and assembly process and is ready to roll. *CHECK*

6   *Now we need to set our engine on its track and receive a fire that can move in and through us and power us toward our life's destiny . . .*

When we speak of *Surrender*, it's important that we clarify what this means to the believer. Typically, when we hear the word *surrender* thoughts of quitting or "throwing in the towel" come to mind, which is exactly what we encouraged *against* in the prior chapter. When the believer hears the term *surrender*, however, an entirely different meaning is to be understood. While there is something relinquished in the act of Christian surrender, it is *not* our hope of victory. It is, in fact, quite the opposite.

When we as believers surrender we are simply transferring *control* of our lives to the One who created us and to whom we belong, allowing us to receive His transforming power and live in His freedom. While we must do our part to remain obedient while enduring the trials that will strengthen us, surrendering to God (including Jesus and the Holy Spirit) proves our trust in Him and acknowledges that He alone is our greatest friend and the sole Source of our help.

Furthermore, we come to an understanding that our power (even on our best days) is limited and that we can realize our potential and reach our purpose destinations *only* with His power moving in and through us. To receive the fullness of God's grace and freedom, we must understand that the purpose of this life is not about seeking control through the illusion of independence but rather about relinquishing control in dependence on the One who has already won on our behalf the freedom we desire. In that process (called sanctification) we become more like Him as His Spirit power breaks us free from the enemy's chains and lies about who we are, his promise of worldly treasure, and the temporary satisfaction of our fleshly cravings.

I have found that *living* in Surrender, however, is the hardest as it requires two choices, which involve inviting and depending on a power from the Holy Spirit. The first choice is to *believe* truth and let go of the enemy's lies that chain us to our lesser selves (keep us functioning in the flesh) so that we can faithfully move toward our God-given destiny.

The second choice is to *receive* supernatural power and allow, through daily dependence, the transformative work of God's Holy Spirit to move in and through our lives to reveal our higher selves (in the Spirit) and lead us to delivering our God-intended impact on this world. Before we can take either of these steps, we must make the choice to stop running from that purpose to which our Creator has called us.

THE CENTURY RIDE

In February of 2023 God presented me with an opportunity to make this very decision so that I could take my next steps in living out these *believe* and *receive* steps in my own journey. During September of 2022 I was invited by a friend to participate in a one-hundred-mile cycling event to raise money for cancer research. This event was the thirteenth Miami Dolphins Challenge Cancer Century Ride, and while I could take an entire chapter to detail this journey from preparation to execution, I'll stick to the high points that ultimately moved me toward an act of surrender that would significantly change my life as I knew it.

During the five months leading up to this February 2023 event (and probably another handful of months prior to that, if I'm being completely honest), I had begun to feel an unquestionable stirring in my soul that Common Sail was not the ultimate purpose destination God had in mind for me. While I had grown so much in the past couple of years with the opportunity I had been given to lead our business, I knew that I wasn't using to the fullest the gifts God had given me for kingdom impact. The more I prayed about this undeniable pull toward something beyond, the more I found myself imagining what a future in consulting, using my gifts to coach, lead, speak, and teach, might look like.

The past six years had added so much to my knowledge of leadership and of business in general, and I kept envisioning what a future of impacting lives through equipping teams and leaders across industries might entail. At the same time life was good right where we were at. We had survived COVID and had our business moving in the right direction. The quarterly bonuses that reflected that success weren't so bad, either. So, as the weeks passed and the getaway that Samantha and I had planned around this race event for our nineteenth wedding anniversary drew closer, I continued to wrestle with God about what the next right step in my life and career should be.

I eventually arrived in Miami and successfully completed my participation in the Century Ride. While completing this ride was exhausting, it was an incredibly rewarding experience that tested my physical endurance, proved God's miraculous power. and gave me some much needed time to be alone with, rely on, and listen to God for His direction.

Once I had finished the race, Samantha and I headed to Anna Maria Island near Tampa, where she had booked us a week's vacation at a gulf-side resort to celebrate our anniversary. This week ended up being the perfect time for us to reconnect and for me to reflect, without daily stresses and pressures, on what I felt to be a call from God toward which I was being summoned.

Over the course of the week, Samantha and I discussed what I had been feeling and sensing over recent months and began to talk through what the future might look like if I were to leave Common Sail. This was a big deal for us and loaded with unknowns. Yet as the list of uncertainties grew, so did my conviction that I was supposed to be trusting God in a way I had never done before.

After all, if leaving public education for employment in private business had been the equivalent of boarding a ship that was leaving the shoreline, this prospective move would be a lot more like getting out of the boat altogether. Nonetheless, because of our discussions and the still, daily quiet time I spent with God on a waterfront that revealed His incredible sovereignty and majesty, I became convinced, with an unexplainable peace, that I needed to step out of the comfortable boat I was in and move toward Him.

LETTING GO

As I returned home to Michigan, having decided to leave what had become comfortable to me in favor of a call toward my purpose destination, I could sense the enemy attacking the conviction and peace I had felt before we left Anna Maria Island. Once I was back home, the unknowns of supporting a family without having a biweekly paycheck, along with the logistic details relative to starting a business and finding day job employment while I pursued this dream, were very real and caused me to rethink my conviction before having a conversation with Dan, from which I wouldn't be able to walk back. I wondered whether he would be angry or hurt. Would he see me as ungrateful and tell me to have my stuff packed by noon? I didn't have any answers to these questions, and this was nerve-racking.

Additionally, I began to doubt my own ability to be successful in an endeavor like this. My enemy was quick to remind me of the times I had failed in the past, which had led me to second-guess whether the calling God seemed to have made so clear was truly for me. Like Moses in Exodus 3 and 4, I began to negotiate with God, insinuating that maybe He had gotten it wrong this time. Perhaps I could "kind of" do what he called me to, without taking the risk.

That was the point at which God pulled me back into His presence with a much-needed reminder of whose I was and a conviction that belonging to Him meant that He would always be in control. Not only that, but He had already given me everything I would need to be successful, including the power of His Holy Spirit. This gave me the assurance I needed to step forward in bold faith that He would work all things together for my good and provide for any pursuit toward which He was calling me.

I made the choice to let go of what I had been holding on to and to trust Him. He then relieved my anxiety over how I would engage in the necessary upcoming conversations with a reminder that He had already won my victory; all I needed to do was stand firm and speak humbly and confidently from the conviction I was no longer going to fight.

With a renewed belief in my calling to fully utilize my gifts and leverage my passions in pursuit of unlocking others in their best-version pursuits, I was ready to open the conversation with Dan. As it turned out, Dan proved to be a friend in that dialogue.

While acknowledging that my timing was not ideal from a business perspective, he validated my gifts to speak to, coach, mentor, and equip leaders. He then expressed his need for some time to think about next steps for the business. I exhaled with gratitude as I walked away from his office. By God's grace our first hurdle had been cleared. There was still much to be resolved, but none of the possible "worst case scenarios" I had feared would come remotely close to playing out.

In a fashion that was true to form for Dan, in less than twenty-four hours he had formulated a plan for taking next steps. When I got to his office I took a seat. "JB," he opened with a grin, "I think I have a way forward for our business and for you to pursue this Jesus calling of yours."

"Great," I replied.

"Are you still interested in moving to the Grand Rapids area?" he asked.

"Well, that depends," I hedged. "With the uncertainty this change could create, I'm not sure it's the best time."

"Makes sense," he replied. "Here's what I think we should do. In the past twenty-four hours I've talked to your peer leaders in the business, and they all said they would want their people to be coached and mentored by you. So, . . . why don't we become your first client? You could set up a space in our Grand Rapids office and maintain an occasional presence there, and it probably makes more sense for you to stay on a W2 while we work through this transition over the course of the next year or so."

I couldn't believe my ears. This was surely too good to be true! God was honoring my decision to faithfully follow His call on me without any tangible worldly promises by opening unimaginable doors and making possible a way for my wholehearted pursuit of His dream for me! All I had to do was sit back and watch it all unfold. I was beyond grateful.

Over the course of the next few months, I transitioned out of my old role. By the end of July Samantha and I had bought and moved into a new home in Zeeland, Michigan. This entire whirlwind happened so fast that it gave me plenty of practice in releasing control and trusting God. It was in that willingness to let go and take those next steps in faith, without regard for how others might be perceiving my decision, that I was able to begin to see God at work, performing miracle after miracle, as circumstances fell so seamlessly into place.

Summer ended, and Landon and Ellie were quick to make friends at their new schools, while Izzy started her freshman year at Michigan State, having enjoyed a summer of exploring and visiting Lake Michigan beaches.

Once things quieted down I began to realize just how far from the boat I had ventured. My phone, which had been a 24/7 source of activity, was now mostly silent. My email account that had been flooded with business updates, problems to solve, and appointment requests was now far less active. As the month of September was ending I had yet to secure any new clients for my Captain's Light Consulting business (co-named by Landon), and I wasn't sure where I'd find the time to address this while coaching thirty plus Common Sail leaders and facilitating on-site team training sessions.

Despite all that God had provided to this point, both in terms of safely delivering my family and me from one life situation into the next and quickly introducing us to people and resources that allowed us to begin making a true home in our new town, I began to wonder, *Did I do the right thing here?*

IGNITING A FIRE

On Sunday morning, September 24, 2023, I decided to take this mounting anxiety to God in prayer. As usual He met me there, took on the weight of my cares, and refocused my attention. After my prayer time had ended I decided to head out to our patio to enjoy a crisp fall Sunday morning. During that time, I thought I would drop an encouraging text to anyone God might choose to place upon my heart that day. That person turned out to be Harlon Barnett, who had recently been named Interim Head Football Coach at Michigan State following the sudden removal of the previous head coach.

After having started the season 2–0, the Spartan football team had suffered convincing losses in their next two games. Assuming that Harlon was carrying a heavy load, I sent him a quick text letting him know that I was praying for him and would be happy to serve if needed. He responded within the hour, enthusing, "Your timing is perfect, Jeremy. Can you talk to our team in Iowa this Friday night at the hotel before our Saturday game?" I immediately said yes.

In a follow-up conversation that week Harlon mentioned that the primary goal for him and the staff at that time was to keep the "train on the tracks"; it was from this conversation that the railroad metaphor to run alongside my Identity and Mentality content was born. My theme for the talk was going to be "I AM," precisely as in a vision for the message that had begun to materialize in my mind years earlier. Over the course of the next couple of days, I went to work to build a PowerPoint slide deck that I would present as a visual accessory for my talk with the team, complete with the newly formed rock-bed foundation and railroad track metaphor in place.

On that Friday evening, September 29, 2023 (also my forty-fourth birthday), I pulled into the parking lot at the team hotel with my son, Landon, for whom Harlon had also secured a game ticket. I was both excited and a bit anxious to get this talk underway. The excitement stemmed from the fact that I have always loved my alma mater and my old football program; sharing this experience now with my son on my birthday took it all over the top.

The anxiety, on the other hand, centered around the fact that I was six years removed from the last time that I had addressed a sports team, and ten years removed from speaking to a division 1 football team before they were to compete with an opponent in the arena, was also there. Nonetheless, we grabbed our bags from the car and headed into the hotel to check into our room before delivering the talk.

As I was waiting for the desk attendant to finish making our room keys, I glanced at the wall behind me and saw what served for me as a small but significant sign of assurance from God on a generic piece of framed hotel wall art. The close-up, black-and-white photo in that frame was of a train charging forward on its tracks. At that moment anxiety disappeared, and it was all a joy ride from there. After Landon and I had deposited our bags in our room we returned to the lobby, where I was able to catch up with some familiar coaches before the team arrived at the hotel ballroom where I'd be providing their message.

Once the talk began I reminded these young men that their true value and worth were defined by the supernatural force that sustained them rather than by the media and fans who were heavily criticizing them. We then discussed what competing with a Conqueror's Mentality might look like and how they could move forward with that mindset in the following day's game.

When the talk was finished several players and coaches approached the front of the hotel ballroom to introduce themselves. The ensuing conversations served as confirmation that the intended message had landed. The next morning after the team breakfast, I had the chance for a more in-depth conversation with a couple of the players before they headed toward the stadium.

The team carried with them into the arena a sixty-minute fight that night. While they lost a heartbreaker, they had played well in a tough road environment against a nationally ranked team, and I was confident that the talk played at least a small part in their resilient effort.

With my mind fully awake and active and my son as my travel companion, I decided to drive back home that night. We discussed the highs and lows of the game, and he even opened a video that he had taken from the back of the hotel ballroom of my talk the night before.

"That was pretty cool," Landon said, to which I responded, "Yeah, it sure was, Lando." It had been cool for me, too, not just as a Spartan alum but because my son had enjoyed the opportunity to experience it with me. The situation was priceless. From nearly as far back as I could remember, I'd had a passion for the game of football. Rarely had a situation presented itself, whether in school, life, or business, that didn't suggest some parallel to a lesson learned through the sport. I realized that weekend that my passion for this game and for the young men who competed in it was still strong. I knew that I had to do something with this.

In the time between that weekend and the conclusion of the 2023 college football season, I reached out to several contacts of mine either still in, or recently departed from, the world of college football. My curiosity was met with generosity by each of them as they shared their input and insights. Two things became clear after those conversations: (1) There was a need for messages like these in this space, and (2) there were some significant barriers to entry to overcome. Nonetheless, the initial validation was all I needed to begin exploring a pursuit.

As February of 2024 approached, I looked back on what had been one full year since my decision to surrender control in my career in favor of pursuing a calling my Creator had placed on my life. I was reminded of His faithfulness and could see how He was using this season in my life to redeem and apply so many prior experiences and relationships. From teaching to coaching and from leading in schools to leading in business (not to mention personal life lessons learned through challenges aside from my career), I could see how His hand had been preparing me for whatever He had in store for me. While that picture had not become crystal clear to me yet, I could sense the aligning that would assist in revealing that specific vision.

One of those significant pieces was the church home Samantha and I selected for our family. This body of believers was Hope Church in our new hometown of Zeeland, Michigan. While Samantha and I had tried other churches in our area in recent months, Hope Church was the place in which we sensed the greatest fit, and we were quickly given opportunities to contribute, serve, and be a part of the overall mission of the church.

Additionally, through an unforeseen chain of events, that pastor (Dave) was then serving as "Coach Dave" at Landon's high school. While I had admittedly made football (the character of the coaching staff and the scheme of play) a variable in deciding where Landon would attend school, I had not known Dave at that time. It was only after the head coach we had previously met submitted a surprising June resignation that Dave assumed this position. This was one more blessing and sign of God's providence at work in our circumstances, and I was grateful for this new friendship that would both challenge and strengthen me and provide a quality example of a Christ-following leader for my son.

As I persisted during this season of change, learning how to allow the Holy Spirit to power me forward, God helped me become a person of greater love, joy, peace, patience, kindness, goodness, faithfulness, gentleness, and self-control (Galatians 5:22–23) in each new relationship I established. As this happened I could feel myself growing in strength and confidence, knowing that, if I would continue to remain focused and pair my hard work with trust in Him, I would arrive at the place and destiny toward which He was guiding me and experience the redeeming victory He had dreamed for me—all in His perfect timing.

LETTING GOD

During this time I was also learning what it meant to truly "walk with God" and surrender daily. For so much of life I had viewed my times with God as the equivalent of "corner experiences" in boxing. He was in the place where I needed to catch a breath and get my wounds cared for before my return to the ring to fight— on my own. I now realized in my total Surrender that He had been right there *with* me all along, even *in* the ring, so to speak.

The same is true for you! He wants you to live your life paired with and dependent upon Him. While our culture teaches that freedom is found in our independence, the Spirit reveals that true freedom is found only in *complete dependence* upon God. It is only through surrender that we can be set free and liberated from what enslaves and imprisons us. Why? Because it is God's truth that sets our souls free, and that truth can be found only in Him, through His Word, which is discerned for us by His Spirit.

While it's not up to us to determine or even predict how He will bring us over, around, or through the obstacles we face in life (Exodus 13 and 14), it is our responsibility to decide whether we will trust Him. When we decide to relinquish our control and let God's power move in and through us, He carries us to our destiny. When we understand this truth and receive the power of His Holy Spirit, we are *transformed* into people who resemble Him and can experience, to its maximum potential, His promise for our lives and become free indeed.

REINVENTING A CAREER

During the winter months of 2024, I began to take steps toward presenting a message and a mentoring curriculum (rooted in I AM principles) to Division 1 football decision-makers, thanks to connections and friendships made during my time as a student athlete at Michigan State twenty-plus years earlier. While many of those meetings were less than fruitful, one opened a door that led to my first real opportunity to serve in this space. That meeting was with Alabama Football. In addition to receiving feedback on my content, I was booked for a summer 2024 speaking engagement with the program's rookie group (freshmen and first-year transfers). Following that Tuscaloosa visit I met with a couple of other programs in the Carolinas that also provided encouragement.

While riding that high I decided to visit a place the history teacher in me had always wanted to see: Kitty Hawk, North Carolina. This was where the famous Wright brothers had achieved the first flight in human history. After driving eastward across the state of North Carolina following my last campus visit, I crossed the Virginia Dare Memorial Bridge that led me to the oceanside hotel on the Outer Banks that I would call home for that evening. After treating myself to some local "High Cotton BBQ" for dinner, I crashed early, anticipating what I'd learn about the Wright brothers' story the following day.

Before I checked out of my hotel the following morning I took in an incredible sunrise on the Atlantic Ocean beachfront with my audience of One and then headed for the Wright Brothers national park at Kill Devil Hill. As I moved closer to the center of the park I noticed a monument titled "Conquest of Air," shaped like a mighty wing and invoking thoughts of the brothers' undaunted courage and undeterred conviction in their pursuit.

Later, while walking through the museum, I learned that upon arriving in Kitty Hawk in 1900 (after having left their native Dayton, Ohio, for better atmospheric conditions and a sandy landing pad), the brothers had continued to endure failure and discouragement that even led Wilbur, in 1901, to suggest that they give up. Fortunately, Orville, anchored by hope and a certainty that the vision God had instilled in their hearts would come to pass, did not agree.

While the brothers had quickly resolved their challenges regarding control and steering (learned through their laboring as bicycle mechanics in Dayton) and lift (learned through their observance of wind's effects), they struggled mightily in addressing the issues regarding thrust and power. How did they engage these challenges? First, they built a track. Yep. Just like on a railroad. The track helped elevate their flyer off the thick sand so they could build momentum.

After developing a lightweight solution for powering their dual propellers in late 1903, their patience in the process finally paid off. All that was left to do was for Orville to lie down and Wilbur to release the track chain as they *surrendered* to the Force that contributed His wing-lifting wind to carry their flyer into flight, just as He had done for the birds the brothers had observed before they had begun their quest. No matter what pursuits we are engaged in, there is so much to learn from the Wright brothers' story. I, personally, would need to recall it for inspiration during the ensuing weeks of my pursuit.

During May and June 2024 I pressed on and delivered on engagements I had acquired (most significantly, the Rookie talk at Alabama Football). Ironically, at the same time other doors from the Carolina schools that had once showed great promise were closing. This was discouraging, not to mention that my current contract arrangement with Common Sail was ending. While I wasn't in full panic mode, I was close. So, I doubled down on disciplined persistence in prayer, praise, focus, and work as I obediently persevered, with belief, through the doubt that was prone to attack me whenever I lost sight of who, and whose, I was.

It was during one of these times that I thanked God for His countless blessings on my life and asked Him to examine my heart and purify my intentions. In response, He returned me to the place where this vision had begun to unfold and recentered my focus on what it was all about: doing my part to share God's light and love with others so that His kingdom might be seen and experienced on earth, as it is in heaven. By His grace He then renewed my conviction and gave me the strength and patience to wait for Him to move.

MAKING A WAY

Within the next two weeks three significant developments transpired. First, Dan called and asked if I'd extend my arrangement with Common Sail. He wanted to engage my insights and expertise on a couple of projects and opportunities for the StoryPoint business. My answer: Yes! Second, I had a discussion with the CEO of a local construction company with whom I had built a relationship over the prior six months. He wanted to contract with me to run the leaders in his company through my leader development program, as he was looking to successfully scale his company's growth. Again, my answer was "Absolutely!"

Then finally, Dave (my pastor, friend, and the Holland Christian football coach) asked me to consider devoting a couple of days per week to coaching quarterbacks for the football program during the upcoming season. After examining the calendar I responded in the affirmative. As a cherry on top, he even asked if I'd deliver a Conqueror's Way talk for a men's event at our church *and* deliver a Sunday morning message to the entire congregation. By the end of July my cup was overflowing with opportunities to serve others in alignment with my calling and vision. These developments didn't happen in the way or timeframe I had expected, but they happened.

Now, as I write the end of this book at forty-five years of age, I still don't know how far my Conqueror's Way message or Captain's Light mentoring will reach. What I do know is that my sights are set in the direction of His calling for me and that, with

His lifting grace, there's no telling how high both can soar and how far His impact through this calling might reach.

Also, despite the discomfort that has come with this new way of living, I've personally experienced a lasting peace, joy, and freedom (through walking daily in a personal relationship with Christ) I'd never known before. As I remain focused on Him, the doubts and fears that once clouded my outlook are relegated to my rearview. While concerns still surface, I continue to practice taking captive false thoughts and making them obedient to God's truth. In all of this I have seen God provide blessings beyond my limited earthly perception of what is possible.

Looking back over my journey to this point, I am filled with gratitude for every single door that He has opened . . . and for the doors he has closed on my behalf along my pursuit of Him. While this story is far from complete and my work far from done, I have found an assured contentment in His truth and have become more and more willing to be clay in the hands of a God who, by His mercy, Spirit, and power, wants and patiently waits for my surrender so that He can mold and shape me into His image for what He has put me on this earth to do. I have also seen God miraculously redeem countless missteps and mistakes I have made through the years, restore to me the joy of His salvation, and renew a fire to share His light and love with others through using the unique gifts He has given me.

Yet, while His redeeming work has been amazing to behold in so many ways, there will likely always remain one "do-over" I wish I could re-play. That is to have placed on the table earlier my wholehearted surrender to my loving Creator. If I'm being totally honest, in fact, to have taken this step *first*. The truth is that, somewhere along the way, I traded in the childlike faith He asked of me for the fleeting and unsatisfying promises of this world—and in so doing wasted years (while sleepwalking in religious exercise) that belonged to Him and could have revealed more of His wonder in my own life.

While His wonderful grace has been sufficient to cover for my human error, as He has worked all these things miraculously for my good, I want everyone who reads this to understand that there was no single event that incited me to relegate my Savior to the tiny box to which I had assigned Him. Instead, this squelching of His influence in my life happened unknowingly, gradually over time, with each small decision I decided to make on my own, apart from His wisdom and according to my own understanding. It wasn't until I chose to put Him first that He became not only my *Savior* but the *Lord* of my life, and it is only in this position that He could truly direct my path.

In humbly walking His Way I have come to experience that *peace* is found in His unchanging love and in the awareness of His constant presence; *joy* is found in experiencing and sharing Jesus's guiding light (through relationships and overcoming trials); and *freedom* is discovered in dying to self and living with Him through His indwelling Holy Spirit, who gives me the power I need to daily conquer my flesh in pursuit of His dream for me. Therefore, in thanksgiving for all I've been given, I'll strive to honor my God with every breath, heartbeat, and step, to further the sharing of the Good News of His kingdom on earth.

Now, as we bring this book to a close, I want to encourage you to do the same. That is, to wholeheartedly make Jesus Christ your Savior *and Lord*, through complete surrender to Him and His will for your life. Why? For starters, the world needs God's intended version of you now more than ever! Also, so that you can begin to experience the fullness of life He intended for you that brings you the peace, joy, and freedom your soul longs for. Although putting Him first in your frenetic, chaos-crazed twenty-first-century life won't be easy, I can promise you it *will* be worth it. And the best news is that you don't have to be a religious scholar or theologian to know it. Our loving God has made walking in His Way SIMPLE for people just like you and me!

As you may have noticed, the key themes of this book happen to lay out in a "simple" to recall pneumonic (memory) device, an acrostic or acronym for you to use should you choose to make God's calling on your life your top priority, today . . .

Surrender
Identity
Mentality
Purpose
Links
Endurance

While there is nothing magical about this device, it can serve to set our expectations for the key opportunities this life will present to us along the way to our purpose destinations. Whether coaching young men on a football field or adults from both genders in all walks of life, I have learned that we all play the game of life at our confident best when the concepts we're trying to live out are simple to recall and implement. Therefore, I encourage you to reset your life's journey upon the Conqueror's Way, using the SIMPLE framework outlined in this book.

Railroad Metaphor Final: Powered by Holy Spirit Fire

There are comparisons to be made between the way old-time locomotives were powered and how God wants to power our purpose pursuits. As mighty as the early locomotives were, they required a power source beyond the potential in their mighty engines to move them toward their destinations. Similarly, we need the fire of God, fueled by the mystery of His grace, to move us toward our purpose destinations. To attempt to go it alone is the equivalent of trying to power a locomotive with a candle. It simply won't work.

After coming to this understanding, we must receive His Holy Spirit fire that purifies our intentions, gives us wisdom, increases our capacity, sharpens our focus, and powers our actions so that our purpose can be served through His empowering might. We create space for this fire by letting go of the variables beyond our control that so easily occupy our energy and attention.

This fire must then be continually fed through our disciplined and obedient daily choices. This is an ongoing process (like an engine fireman shoveling coals into an old-fashioned boiler). If our fire is fed by the approval and applause of others, it is not the fire of the Holy Spirit and will eventually die out. With me so far?

As we feed the flame, it must be fanned to grow into a blazing inferno powerful enough to propel a locomotive. For those early trains this was accomplished as wind, collecting between the locomotive engine and the rock-bed of the track, breathed through the fire grate, intensifying the fire's heat, boiling the water, and creating pressure. Similarly, the unseen wind operative in our lives as believers can only be God's grace and power. Our effort is required, of course, but it is ultimately through the miraculous and unseen grace of God that His Spirit's fire propels us.

Finally, it is time for the engine to do what it was built to do: charge fearlessly on its tracks toward its destination by harnessing steam pressure to trigger a chain reaction between pistons and rods connected to wheels that initiate forward movement. So it is with our lives.

Many aspects of life create pressure within us. The problem is that, if we don't understand the difference between positive pressure (purpose and reaching our potential) and negative pressure (the opinions of others, insecurity, fear, etc.), we risk increasing our distress and are vulnerable to the devastating effects that internal combustion can have on our physical, mental, spiritual, and emotional well-being. We must learn how to harness the good and release the bad. Once we do this, a redeeming and life-changing transformation results.

SURRENDER TAKEAWAY . . .

God's Supernatural Power Is Required for Enhancing Your Senses and Reaching Your Potential.

God wants us to let go of whatever holds us back so that we can discover our fullest potential in Him and for Him. When you relinquish what holds you back and allow the Holy Spirit's transformational power to move in and through you, God can do exceedingly more through your trust than you could ask, think, or imagine (Ephesians 3:20). Surrendering to His will moves you to the only place where true freedom, which has already been won through the crucifixion and resurrection of Jesus Christ, may be found. As a result of that conquering work, the enemy of your soul and your flesh no longer holds dominion over you, and you are free to move as the Spirit does.

QUESTIONS: What is keeping you from surrendering and from realizing your destiny and victory in Christ? What fuels your pursuits? Is this energy source both powerful and sustainable?

APPLICATION: Consider how operating from your illusion of control has impacted your life and the lives of others around you. Assess what factors currently motivate your goals and pursuits. Decide which motives reflect your insecurities and fears, and then begin the practice of surrendering these to your loving heavenly Father and inviting His Holy Spirit to ignite in you motives that are pure and come from a genuine desire to offer your utmost for His highest.

CONCLUSION

WHEELS TO WINGS

"The most beautiful thing we can experience is the mysterious."
ALBERT EINSTEIN

Have you, like the Wright Brothers, observed an eagle fly? These magnificent raptors are the embodiment of freedom, soaring effortlessly and gracefully through the sky in trusting dependence on the One who sustains them and provides the conditions for their flight. In many ways this is what living in communion with the fullness of God (Father, Son, and Holy Spirit in their tri-unity) is like. Personally speaking, I can attest that, since surrendering and spreading my wings, so to speak, to soar in His freedom, my belief in Him has grown, the load of my stress has lightened, my days have gotten brighter, and I've experienced the joy unspeakable and peace beyond understanding I had only heard about earlier.

With that said, I know that the prospect of abandoning a way of life in which you've been conditioned to participate can be scary. I get it. The truth is that, in my natural human moments, when I subconsciously revert to living on autopilot in the daily grind of life I can still feel that fleshly anxiety. Nonetheless, the more God proves himself to me in flight, the easier it gets for me to trust Him and return to His plan for me.

For the rest of this section I'll provide some practical steps for taking flight with God, so that those of you who are interested can start living the life He designed and intended for you. Before I do so, though, I want to transition from the already completed railroad metaphor to a different, concluding analogy.

LEARNING TO FLY

Back when I was traveling around the Midwest region of the United States for work, I had the good fortune of having access to a company jet that could take me as far as Collierville, Tennessee, at start of business (Central Time) for a day with one of our community leaders and teams (and a visit with my favorite resident and Memphian friend, Marvin Ford) and then home for dinner with my family in Michigan by 6:00 p.m. Eastern Standard Time.

As much as I appreciated this luxury, I also enjoyed getting to know the pilots who flew us around on countless flights. There was one pilot, though, I got to know better than the others. His name was Don Weaver. One day I asked Don, "What are a good pilot's top priorities?"

He responded, "It's actually pretty simple." I liked the sound of that! "Once a certified and licensed pilot has gone through their on-ground checklist, which includes a review of the aircraft manual and flight plan," he shared, "they have three things to prioritize before and during flight: aviate, navigate, and communicate, in that order."

With that intel I decided to create a closing mini-metaphor for living the Conqueror's Way, in flight, in complete partnership and dependence on our loving God, who desires to elevate us above and beyond our forward-moving tracks and into the great unknown of His mysterious and rarified air. So, here were go.

CERTIFICATION AND LICENSURE

Before an aspiring pilot is allowed to fly a plane, they must first demonstrate, through training and testing, that they understand the basics of flight. Similarly, before I begin walking us through Don Weaver's flight priorities of aviate, navigate, and communicate, I want to direct your attention to, and suggest your thoughtful reading of, the Bible. In particular the book of Ephesians (found in the New Testament of your *Flight Manual*).

In chapters 1, 2, and 3 of this letter, written by the apostle Paul to the early church in Ephesus (located in modern day Turkey), you'll find a great listing of passages you'll want to become familiar with before taking flight. What I want you to grasp first, before taxiing down your runway, though, is that God chose you and designed a destiny for you that can be fulfilled *only* when you follow the Way of Jesus Christ (the Conqueror's Way), in reliance on the power of His Holy Spirit (Ephesians 1:45).

Your enemy *will* try to deceive you by getting you to believe that you are not capable or "enough." That's a lie. I urge you to get familiar with your Flight Manual so you can quickly recall truth when the enemy attacks. The underlying truth is that God created you intentionally, as a one-of-a-kind masterpiece endowed with the gift of life that He alone authored and designed.

Amazingly, He prepared *in advance* (made provision for) specific good works (Ephesians 2:10) for you to do. He also wants to dwell in your heart so that you may be filled with, and rooted in, His perfect love and possess the fullness of God within you. While this may all sound mysterious and too good to be true, remember who is promising it. Not me, but God (check your Flight Manual for proof)! The same One who authored your life and powers the very breaths and heartbeats that sustain it is able to do immeasurably more than you could ever ask, think, or imagine, according to His power working in and through you (Ephesians 3:17–20)—if you'll just trust Him.

There are a couple more things you'll need to understand before being cleared to fly. The bottom line is that there is *one* prescribed Way to fly (John 14:6). Flying an aircraft is not a trial-and-error experience that anyone should take lightly. While a pilot may have a certain style that is unique to them as a flyer, there are rules for successfully navigating the laws of nature to fly safely and successfully.

The same is true of our lives. There is a way to live safely and successfully, and the same God whose laws of nature create parameters for our physical reality has set boundaries for our emotional, intellectual, and spiritual reality as well. Before we get to those behavior requirements, though, we must never forget this critical truth: the One who chose *you* (Isaiah 42–45) to fly to whatever specific destination He has ordained for you loves you and, as your heavenly Father, is proud of you. He also requires three things from you:

> *To act justly and to love mercy*
> *and to walk humbly with your God.*
> MICAH 6:8

Life will present you with challenges that test your ability to live out these requirements. Once we have passed our test, however, we are ready to receive the flight assignment to our purpose destination. Sometimes God's flight assignments excite us, while at other times they frighten or anger us. Regardless of the circumstances, however, it's in our best interest to accept our assignment with confidence in both our training and in our Appointer. In the book of Matthew Jesus provides good reason to do so:

> *"Are not two sparrows sold for a penny? Yet not one of*
> *them will fall to the ground outside your Father's care.*
> *And even the very hairs of your head are all numbered.*
> *So don't be afraid; you are worth more than many*
> *sparrows."*
> MATTHEW 10:29-31

God has a masterplan for your life, and He wants you to discover it and live it out. Rest assured that every assignment you receive is designed for you to positively impact others by sharing your light at just the right moments, depending on His flawless timing (see Esther 4:12–14 for an illustration of this). If you understand this and can demonstrate that you are able and willing to soar in accordance with this truth, you are ready for flight.

STEP 1: AVIATE (*IN THE HOLY SPIRIT*)

When Don was describing to me Step 1 (aviate) of a pilot's flight priorities, he noted that this step is the most difficult, specifically because the most demanding aspects of aviation are the takeoff and the landing. The atmospheric element that makes these stages of flight challenging is the very force that makes flight possible in the first place—the *wind*. We'll get to that more in a moment.

God wants you to take flight in your life with the blessed assurance that His unfailing and constant love (John 3:16) will always be available to you; not only that, but it will always be more than enough to lift you up and guide your Way (John 1:1–14) when life's forces are pushing against you. Once you understand and *believe* this, it's time to power your jets and begin taxiing toward your assigned runway.

As you begin to build momentum and speed along your runway, don't forget that you should *expect* resistance—but don't worry. You *need* this very resistance to make your lift-off possible. As you gain speed and see your runway shortening, it's time to lift your eyes, raise your steering column, and allow God's wind-providing grace and Spirit to rush beneath you and buoy you up, drawing you closer to His heavenly realm (John 3:8).

One of the aspects of flying I've always enjoyed most is the experience of lift-off. The rush of speed spikes my adrenaline, as I literally feel the earth beneath me being pushed away as the aircraft defies gravity. The experiencing of rising toward God's calling for me creates a similar feeling. Additionally, even though the weather on the ground may be nasty with wind, rain, fog, or snow, there is always a breakthrough point at which we rise above those obstacles and see God's light, which brings clarity as far as our eye can see.

The same experience is true of taking spiritual flight. Our earthly conditions may not be ideal; they may even depress us and/or discourage us from flying, but if we push back against that resistance, leaning on the promises of God, we will see the light . . . and, when we do, the amazing grace that lifted us will overwhelm us with awe over the limitless universe our heavenly Father created and wants us to experience firsthand. Therefore, learn to be grateful for the resistance, even when that isn't easy. There simply is no other way for grace to lift you to flight.

STEP 2: NAVIGATE [*THROUGH* THE SON]

Now that you have successfully accelerated in alignment with your runway, leveraged your resistance, and harnessed the power required for flight, it's time to keep your eyes on the course and follow it. Fortunately, Jesus made the Way to our destination abundantly clear. We navigate our path both by knowing Him and making Him known as we make pursuing God and His kingdom *the* goal of our existence.

When we seek Him and His kingdom destination for us as our top priority, following the fundamental directives Jesus laid out for us of *loving God* and *serving others* (in that order), our source of guidance for our journey is set. Be sure not to overcomplicate this situation as so many do. Your God wants your flight to be safe and successful, which is why he makes the Way so straightforward, so *simple*. Don't let that reality escape you when life gets chaotic and messy. Keep your eyes on Him and the destination he has called you toward, and you *will* arrive safely!

STEP 3: COMMUNICATE [*WITH* THE FATHER]

Now that you are safely gliding through the air, make sure to stay plugged in to communication with your air traffic controller (God), your co-pilot(s), and your passengers. As we begin to prepare this metaphor for landing, I'll touch on each of these three communication partners.

Never forget that your life's destination, and the very air you breathe (Acts 17:28), are set and sustained by God, who is also known as the Alpha and Omega (beginning and ending) of the entire universe in which you reside. Allow Him to establish your plans, as directed in the book of Proverbs:

Commit to the LORD whatever you do,
and he will establish your plans.
PROVERBS 16:3

Make it a regular practice to communicate with Him continuously, trusting Him above all else (Isaiah 2:22). When your enemy taps into your radio frequency and attempts to reinstate the insecurity, doubt, and fear that once enslaved you, through self-limiting internal monologue or the detracting opinions of others, ignore it! The truth is that the moment you surrendered to God and committed to pursuing His Way and purpose for your life, *you* became a conqueror (Romans 6:14) over the enemy of your soul from His position of victory! You have only to call His name when you need Him (in prayer), and He'll remind you of *who* and *whose* you are so you can travel with confidence.

Finally, don't forget to communicate with your co-pilots and the reliable partners you've allowed into your inner circle, as well as the passengers (friends, family, work associates, church acquaintances, neighbors, and community members, etc.) you've been placed on this earth to serve on the way to your purpose destination.

There will be times when you want to reach your destination alone, but this isn't God's design. In the same way He chose the unity and companionship of the Trinity to reveal His fullness, your living in community with others is the only way that the fullest version of yourself, and your intended impact on others, can be realized. Consider this passage from Hebrews as you persevere in the faith:

*[Live this new Way:] Since we have a great priest
(Jesus), . . . let us draw near to God with a sincere
heart and with the full assurance that faith brings,
. . . [cleansed] from a guilty conscience. . . . Let us
hold unswervingly to the hope we profess, for he who
promised is faithful. And let us consider how we may
spur one another on toward love and good deeds, not
giving up meeting together, as some are in the habit of
doing, but encouraging one another—and all the more
as [the day approaches].*

HEBREWS 10:20–25

And with that Paul brings us to the perfect close by
reminding us of Jesus's greatest commandments, which embody
our loving heavenly Father's simplicity that we should not let
escape us: Love God. Serve Others. Living in the experience of
His Victory truly is that . . . Simple.

THE CONQUEROR'S CREED

The Spirit God gave us does not make us timid,
but gives us power, love and self-discipline.
2 TIMOTHY 1:7

1. My *Surrender* frees me from burdens and allows me to let go of what I cannot control. I will trust God and let His truth and transformational power guide me. (Proverbs 3:5–6)

2. My *Identity* is designed by my Creator and is the firm foundation I build my life upon. I will form character and habits to reflect His love and conquer insecurity. (Genesis 1:26–27)

3. My *Mentality* is the thought-track capable of sustaining forward movement in my life. I will cultivate an attitude and mindset of belief to conquer doubt and fear. (Joshua 1:89)

4. My *Purpose* is my destiny, and it calls me to pursue Jesus and make His victory known. I will use my gifts to reveal His light through both word and deed. (Matthew 6:10–34)

5. My *Links* are my network of relationships that I commit to love, serve, and sacrifice for. I will choose wisely which people and partners I connect closely with. (Hebrews 10:24–25)

6. My *Endurance* makes it possible for God's process and my trials to mold and equip me. I will patiently persevere through pain and adversity, with hope, as I grow. (James 1:2–4)

In all these things we are more than conquerors through Him who
loved us.
ROMANS 8:37

I am low in the dust;
Preserve my life according to your word.
PSALM 119:25

"Where, O death, is your victory?
Where, O death, is your sting?"

But thanks be to God! He gives us the victory
through our Lord Jesus Christ.
Therefore, my dear brothers and sisters, stand firm.
Let nothing move you.
Always give yourselves fully to the work of the Lord,
because you know that your labor
in the Lord is not in vain.
1 CORINTHIANS 15:55, 57-58